LESS HELPING THEM
MORE HEALING YOU

Oh, night that guided me,
Oh, night more lovely than the dawn.

St. John of the Cross, *The Dark Night of the Soul*

THE TRANSCENDENT GIFT
OF AN
ANCIENT SPIRITUAL PRACTICE

LESS HELPING THEM
MORE HEALING YOU

JEAN P. KELLY

acta

LESS HELPING THEM / MORE HEALING YOU
The Transcendent Gift of an Ancient Spiritual Practice
Jean P. Kelly

Edited by Gregory F. Augustine Pierce
Cover and text design and typesetting by Andrea Reider
Drawings by Connie Meyer

Text copyright © 2024 by Jean P. Kelly
Artwork copyright © 2024 by Connie Meyer

Unless otherwise noted, Scripture verses are from *New Revised Standard Version, Catholic Edition,* of the Bible, © 1989, 1993 by the Division of Christian Education of the National Council of the Churches of Christ in the United States of America. Used by permission. All rights reserved.

Published by ACTA Publications, 7135 W. Keeney Street, Niles, IL 60714, (800) 397-2282, www.actapublications.com

All rights reserved. No part of this publication may be reproduced or transmitted in any form or by any means, electronic or mechanical, including photocopying and recording, or by any information storage and retrieval system, including the Internet, without permission from the publisher. Permission is hereby given to use short excerpts with proper citation in reviews and marketing copy, institutional bulletins and handouts, and scholarly papers.

Softcover ISBN: 978-0-87946-729-6
Hardcover ISBN: 978-0-87946-734-0

Library of Congress Number: 2024933279

Printed in the United States of America by Total Printing Systems
Year 30 29 28 27 26 25 24
Printing 10 9 8 7 6 5 4 3 2 First
Text printed on 30% post-consumer recycled paper

Dedication

To anyone and everyone who has loved someone addicted, either in the distant past or the painful present.

May you come to recognize in your deprivation the delicate, subtle gifts of grace.

May you trust the dark night to guide your soul toward a dawn that is bright, restorative, and truly transformative.

CONTENTS

Introduction	1
Preview "Stilling" The Destination of Spiritual Reading	13
Step 1 "Shimmering" The Light of Self-Knowledge	27
Step 2 "Settling" When You've Done All You Can	43
Step 3 "Savoring" The Hospitality of Joy	57
Step 4 "Stirring" A Deeper Experience with Poetry and Pilgrimage	71
Step 5 "Summoning" Self-Acceptance through Humility	91

STEP 6
"Serving"
Limits Are Love   109

STEP 7
"Slowing"
Adjusting to Nature's Pace   127

STEP 8
"Stilling"
In a Spiritual Milieu   139

About the Author   155

Acknowledgments   157

APPENDIX 1
Finding and Choosing Texts
for Spiritual Reading   159

APPENDIX 2
Resources for healing from
difficult relationships   163

INTRODUCTION

*Your words became to me a joy
and the delight of my heart,
for I am called by your name.*
Jeremiah 15:16

AT ONE TIME, I pictured myself in a nursing home of the future where family and friends would complain about my pockets full of notes—shreds of paper with handwritten quotes—stashed there and everywhere in case I forgot good advice. I also imagined an avalanche of books, anthologies, and memoirs bristling with post-its, on a bedside stand, never shelved just in case I needed to find, in doubt-filled moments, an inspirational passage, paragraph, or prayer.

Words of others—especially in books—have always offered solace to me: comfort, companionship, escape, insight, and challenge. So when some ten years ago I learned that reading can be prayer, I was hooked. Ever since discovering the ancient spiritual discipline *Lectio Divina*, "Spiritual Reading," I've been on an intentional path back to myself, one page at a time.

That I was lost at all was a surprise revealed over months and years of integrating the method of slow reading, meditation, response, and contemplation into my busy life.

I was only aware I needed a rest, even a momentary escape from the feeling that it was my responsibility alone to navigate my nuclear family of five toward security and success. As the proverb tells us, a journey of a thousand miles begins with the first step, which for me was carving out just fifteen minutes a few days a week for myself. For solitude. For silence. And for reading texts that took me inward, but ones that eventually demanded I make outward changes.

With practice and determination, that "me" time grew to twenty minutes every day. Often before my three daughters and husband awoke, I would ponder my life with a book in my lap. I was still. I listened. Just below my consciousness, I heard a whisper about what was and was not healthy–in my heart, in my soul, and in the relationships where I had invested both.

Loving relationships are gratifying until they're not. But most of us aren't nearly as equipped as we think we are to recognize deep dysfunction without outside input. We hardly hear our own mouths utter the word "but" after we make statements like "I love him" or "She loves me" when what we are really doing is justifying unequal, incomplete,

INTRODUCTION

or manipulative entanglements. If twisted definitions of familial loyalty and responsibility drown out our soul's symphony of needs, we fall back on the ever-present chorus of "helping," "fixing," and "keeping up appearances" with practiced lies and half-truths that say what we have is the best we can hope for.

If control is a familiar tune, we whistle it in the dark. Only our heart hearkens the empty echoes. Spiritual Reading can provide both the space and the grace to un-mute our truest desires and turn up the volume on the truth about love. With time and practice of the eight simple steps in this book, the off-key voices of self-denial can be replaced by sweet harmonies of self-acceptance, which sing alongside the wise guides found in texts of all kinds—including music, art, and life experience. Their refrain is a powerful truth: *genuine love is never earned.*

Spiritual Reading offered me not only a rest stop, but also an unexpected path toward healing that is so remarkable I am compelled now to show others the way. When I fell in love and made a family with an unrepentant alcoholic, I was navigating blind, unable to distinguish signposts toward fulfillment from those pointing toward a toxic mix of old insecurities, self-serving concepts of self-sacrifice, and false humility.

I was detoured for miles and years by patterns of what I now recognize as unhealthy, until I happened upon this ancient approach to mindfulness and the straighter, healthier, spiritual path trod by so many before me. Spiritual Reading taught how to detach from my situation with love in order to experience divine love, accepting that my only obligation to those I loved was mercy, not sacrifice. Once I mastered the technique and became convinced I deserved better, it was easy to get around roadblocks set by the dysfunctional people in my life.

The first steps toward any change are always tentative, often two forward and one back. I've leaned on many spiritual guides along my winding way to wholeness; now I hope you will lean on me until you find your own support, perhaps from professional counseling, setting new boundaries, and developing a deeper connection with the Divine.

Many traditions—including Christianity, Buddhism, Islam, and Judaism—have for centuries believed meaningful internal dialogue and meditation benefit from the external inspiration of reading sacred scriptures or other texts. Even before spiritual seekers were literate, they were often "given a word" by a teacher—often small passages of wisdom memorized, savored. and reflected upon throughout an entire day or even a week. Especially because printed books of psalms and scriptures were often unavailable, religious men and women learned and chanted texts as prayers.

INTRODUCTION

The abbot Saint Benedict of Nursia (founder of the Benedictines) formalized praying and meditating with texts in his monastery in Italy during the sixth century. A structure of the four steps he taught as "movements through mindfulness" were given the Latin names *lectio, meditatio, oratio,* and *contemplatio.* I prefer to call them—in English—*read, reflect, respond,* and *receive.* You'll see those terms at the end of each chapter, along with prompts meant to apply the technique in your own life.

To simplify the practice, I present each of the four "R" steps with two smaller "S" themes, one per chapter, totaling eight: Read—"Shimmering and Settling;" Reflect—"Savoring and Stirring;" Respond—"Summoning and Serving; and Receive—"Slowing and Stilling."

From the start, my approach to the Read step was to choose not scriptural passages as the monastics did, but rather secular texts—fiction, non-fiction, poetry, journalism, stories, essays, and even music and art. Throughout each chapter, as I map my own expedition of the heart, I'll share my favorite guideposts—but only as suggestions of places to start. The appendix offers a longer list of possibilities for you but, more importantly, it is a guide for how to find your own unique inspirational reading.

My own Spiritual Reading journey began with favorite books from my past, which lead to biographies of kindred souls from my Catholic faith tradition, which then lead me, kicking and screaming, to the Hebrew-Christian Scriptures. I was always wary of a Bible-quoting guides inclined to substitute sanctimony and finger-wagging for acceptance, but I set my biases aside once I discovered the Old Testament poets, the mostly anonymous authors of the psalms. Not only were the stanzas perfect bite-size length for my daily meditation, but they expressed emotions I was experiencing: fear, desperation, and anguish, alongside words of praise and rejoicing. They echoed the ever-changing pitches of my own heart song.

For the "reading" step, I left entirely to chance which words to devour, letting my hand select a random title from a shelf and then open the book to any page. (This seeming random choice is a strong part of the tradition). I delighted in finding meaning that way, revealed obliquely perhaps, but no less effectively. What mattered most was that I cultivated an openness to mystery. With that disposition, surprising lessons became available to me, whether they were taught, for example, by brutal outcomes suffered by misfit characters in Flannery O'Connor stories or calls to action that were shouted by activist Dorothy Day or presented in staccato stanzas of Beat poets from the 1960s. No matter the genre of writing, I always stumble upon what I need when I need it.

Perhaps my favorite characteristic of reading as mindfulness is its inherent forgiveness, apparent in the second R: the Reflect movement. I had failed at traditional forms of Eastern meditation thanks to the perpetual anxiety that buzzes just below the surface of any household occupied by an active addict. I could not quiet my thoughts until I discovered Spiritual Reading. As one modern monk writes, "memories or thoughts are simply parts of yourself that, when they rise up during *Lectio Divina,* are asking to be given to God along with the rest of your inner self."

The only goal of Spiritual Reading is the third R: Receptivity. So now, even if heartache muddles my thinking and letters on the page swirl amidst tears, insights are still accessible. If I cannot focus and must read a sentence over and over, that is not an error. The technique dictates reading small selections of any text four times, slowly, each with a slightly different focus. If I can't manage that, I stop and re-read or re-listen or look again at any text that "shimmers" with a connection to my own life. The goal is not analysis and not understanding, but rather something in between. Some adherents of the ancient spiritual discipline call this "holding the passage lightly."

The next step is Respond—what some call "prayer"—which is accessible to me through journaling or writing. I don't understand a text until I digest it with my pen. Flannery O'Connor once wrote, "I write because I don't know what I think until I read what I say." Gervase Holdaway in *The Oblate Life* compares reading as prayer to "feasting" on texts, first taking of a bite of a small passage, chewing on it, savoring its essence, and finally making it a part of the body and mind. Words of others become part of me only after I parse and pair them with my own, triangulating a path of wisdom toward spiritual enlightenment.

I've always appreciated Saint Ambrose's definition of prayer: "Prayer should accompany the reading of sacred scripture, so that God and humans may talk together; for 'we speak to him when we pray; we hear him when we read the divine saying.'" After reading and reflecting, I sometimes address my higher power with gratitude, saying, "Thank you for drawing close to me. You've answered my longings with these words." Though it took many conversations, my divine interlocutor convinced me that, though broken, I am accepted, blessed, and loved unconditionally.

During the last movement, "Receive," I am quiet. I listen. What I hear in my mind's concert hall is not always a symphony, nor is it lightning-bolt revelation. Instead, I take comfort in simply being heard. Spiritual Reading reminds us that the path to happiness is never searching, but being found. The purpose is not to attain mastery, but only to allow the Divine to master us. Even without experiencing deep contemplation every time, I end each session knowing some new wisdom now *belongs* to me: that *any* phrase, *any* sentence, and *any* experience in daily life has the power to show me the way.

Which is why, by the time I end up in that imagined nursing home, my heart will have incorporated the rhythms of this ancient practice, recognizing in every moment what is sacred. I will no longer need those scraps of paper in my pockets.

INTRODUCTION

In today's wired world, knowledge seems available with just a few keywords and clicks. We satisfy any curiosity instantaneously. Momentary confusion or insecurity can be eased just as readily by queuing up a social media app. But rather than a quest for information or to "get something" out of a text, whether a novel or a self-help article on the Internet, Spiritual Reading is counter cultural. It is slow and must begin with an attitude of surrender. Such openness allows for a progression through an ancient spiritual practice that is organic, accepting, and not rigid.

It is not possible to move through the four steps of *Lection Divina* incorrectly. As Australian monk Michael Casey explains, "Sometimes the steps of the ladder are not chronologically connected. Some people combine reading, reflection, and prayer in a single 'exercise;' others separate them in time and space. Many experience a delayed reaction. The impact of their *practice* may strike months later. There is a lot of flexibility here that takes seriously different characters, different vocations, different opportunities, and the changing seasons of life."

With that in mind, to summarize the basic movements of the Spiritual Reading method:

READ

Establish a consistent time and place for reading and reflection. When you begin, prepare your heart and mind by first breathing deeply and slowly. Know that you deserve this time of rest. Then choose just a few lines from a novel, a poem, a song, or details of a work of art. Savor the words, rhythms, and symbols, unhurriedly.

REFLECT

Read again, listening for a word or phrase that is meant for you on this day. Gently turn the passage or image over in your mind, allowing it to interact with thoughts, hopes, memories, and desires.

RESPOND

After reading the passage again, open your heart. Allow your soul to be inflamed by what you sincerely need at this moment. Ask. This can be what some consider prayer, or a written response from you.

RECEIVE

Read the words one last time, then listen. In a spirit of silence and of awe, attend the still, small voice of love and wisdom. It speaks not loudly, but intimately, with a message for you alone.

INTRODUCTION

These four steps need to be done together during each single session. The total time is dependent on the time you have available—from a minimum of perhaps twenty minutes to a maximum of an hour. Each of the four steps should take approximately the same amount of time.

The point is not to become a slave to the time nor the process, however. The goal is to follow with intention an ancient path that leads you to self-knowledge, then self-acceptance, and ultimately self-love. Upon arriving at that destination, you will find both grace and healing enough to love differently and to accept a love that is infinite and perfect, as a daughter or son of the Divine.

May you experience many blessings along this new path.

Jean P. Kelly
Columbus, Ohio
National Co-Dependency Month
January 2024

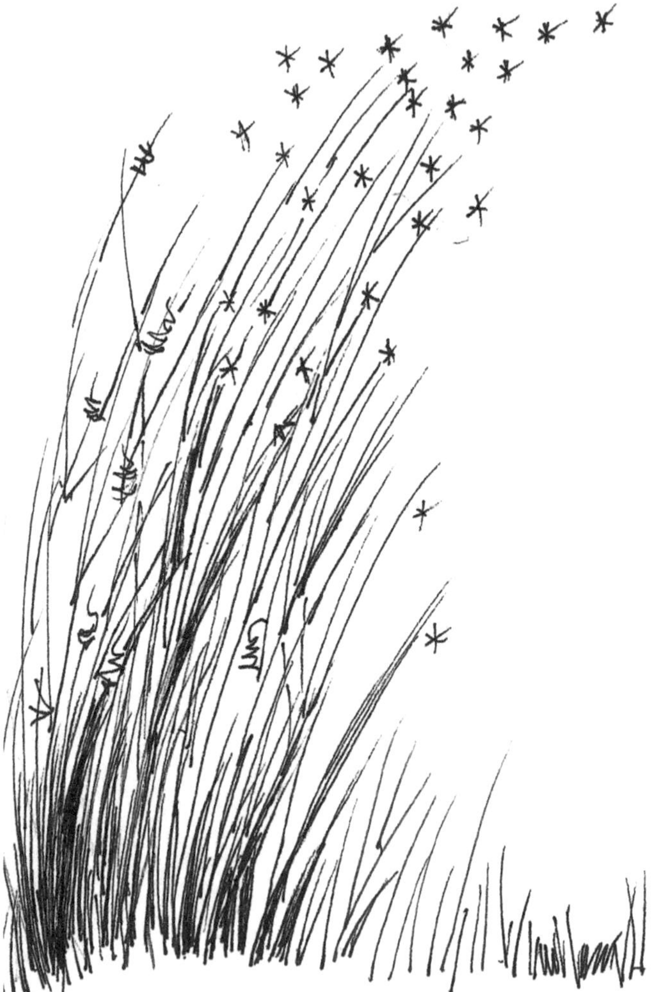

PREVIEW

"STILLING" THE DESTINATION OF SPIRITUAL READING

> Stay clear of those vexed in spirit.
> Learn to linger around someone of ease
> Who feels they have all the time in the world.
> Gradually, you will return to yourself,
> Having learned a new respect for your heart
> And the joy that dwells far within slow time.
>
> John O'Donohue, *For One Who Is Exhausted, A Blessing*

I SIT ON A damp wooden bench on a clover-covered island, surrounded on either side by a rushing, Guinness-colored river. The babble cradles my ears and slows my breathing. I inhale, almost tasting the sweet stench of roots that form cave-like hideaways under trees along the banks. Surely I've found the homes of faeries, so common in the lore of this country. Earthen walls form a cacophonous cocoon around me, blocking the view of the valley as it winds toward the strand and the Kenmare Bay. For both that unseen horizon and my narrow hiding place, I offer gratitude. Then I release all thoughts, all questions, and all self-judgment.

When I first tried meditation like the one above, my goal was to calm a relentless inner vibration that started after I filed for divorce and grew stronger when my then husband dug in his heels and refused to move out of our hapless houschold for nine months until I relented and left. In desperation, I ordered a DVD short course on Centering Prayer. With a portable player, I retreated to my miles-away office alone, at all hours of the day or night—anytime I could excuse my whereabouts.

Faithful to the instructions for the course, I took deep breaths along with the peaceful people on the screen until the spirit suggested a single sacred word that signified my surrender to a higher power. I heard in my heart *"grace."* Although I am a lifelong Catholic, that word's meaning has always eluded me; but I liked its wise, wistful pronunciation. But even repeating such a beautiful one-syllable would not stop my racing thoughts from their assault. I could not empty my mind as instructed. I could not be still.

"STILLING" THE DESTINATION OF SPIRITUAL READING

Stilling is the last step of the spiritual reading technique I first learned years before I needed it most to understand the unearned suffering that comes with loving someone who abuses substances. The simple movements of Spiritual Reading practice lead to Stilling, a final destination along an intentional path. I often imagine myself back in the place where I first found both rest and authentic stillness: an island in a river in southern Ireland.

Travel as part of an academic sabbatical project was approved soon after I decided that decades of second chances was more than enough for a man who felt entitled to drink to excess routinely. I couldn't have imagined then that two bitter years later, when it came time to leave for more than a month at a County Cork writers' retreat, I'd still be married and with no legal arrangement for the shared custody and support of our three teenage daughters.

Every attorney-activated status conference and court hearing between my husband and me ended in stalemate, my proposals for resolution were ignored, and my daughters had no better option than co-dependent chaos. They didn't seem to mind when their father returned home early Sunday mornings after Saturday nights out, passing the rest of his family in the garage as we left for church. It was painful to watch my girls repeat a pattern I knew too well: deciding his behavior was unacceptable; then building tolerance until indifference, manipulation and emotional warfare felt justified; and then, finally taking on his responsibilities as the only viable solution.

Buying groceries with their own money and scheduling their own orthodontist appointments became routine for my daughters, facts they hid from me after I moved out. Left home alone for days while her father left town for a beach vacation, my youngest paid classmates with licenses to taxi her from our rural home to high school. She congratulated herself for self-reliance. Learning of all this after the fact, my gallows sense of humor suggested as dysfunctional family motto my daughters' most common refrain: "It's no big deal, mom."

Because I worried that unanticipated domestic drama might derail my travel plans, I opted to inform my daughters of my six-week international trip just a few days in advance. Returning to transatlantic travel for the first time in decades was fraught with self-doubt. For years I was sure that staying close to home, travelling only in the states for work, was necessary to protect my children.

My husband rarely, if ever, joined me for trips where I presented a paper or picked up an award, having no interest in entertaining himself in the meantime. So I'd fly to a conference and back as quickly as possible. The nagging and criticizing I meted out the moment I saw the mess that had accumulated in my absence was nothing compared to the self-flagellation of "shouldn't-haves" I heaped upon myself. The self-inflicted charge that it was self-centered to travel on my own made me less likely to do so the next time. I even developed a fear of flying, terrified that if the worst happened to me my daughters would be left in the care of a father whose idea of quality time with them included all-day tailgate parties and other sporting events were he could drink with impunity and then drive them home

As Melody Beattie wrote in her classic book *Co-dependent No More*, those of us in relationships with the addicted "are engaged in a form of punishment designed to keep us feeling anxious, upset, and stifled. We trap ourselves."

Though I considered myself to be self-reliant and independent, I had in fact fallen victim to what therapist Colette Dowling calls the "Cinderella Complex." She theorizes that women in particular, even those healthy when they begin relationships with dysfunctional people, fall into a trap dug deeper by staying too long. We eventually feel not just unloved, but unlovable. In exchange for what appears to be security, we agree to settle for a life that is just "good enough." We trade safety for momentary stability, learning to placate and sacrifice to achieve what seems like normalcy.

Beattie put it this way: "Many of us expect and need other people so much that we settle for too little. We may become dependent on troubled people—alcoholics and others with problems." As an antidote, this therapist recommends not self-reliance nor independence, but what she calls "un-dependence."

In the early days of my search for peace, I registered for a one-day spiritual retreat called "Unbound: Forgiveness in the Name of Jesus." In a matter of hours I went from being convinced it was my job to forgive my husband to realizing I needed only to forgive myself. Retreat leaders exposed lies I had crafted in order to cope, such as "I am in control" and "Something is wrong with me" and "God wanted this to happen to me."

In response to their questions, I began to probe long-repressed hurts and patterns of thoughts and behavior by recalling who I had been as a child, a technique also used by psychologists to unearth and treat generational trauma. The retreat was heart-wrenching and confusing to me, but it ended with my first experience of guided meditation.

As prompted by the facilitator's soothing voice, I closed my eyes and journeyed to a calm place of my choosing—a beach. There, I was told to imagine Christ speaking, directly and intimately, these words to me: "Jean, you are a divine daughter of God." For one achingly fleeting moment, the proximity of the Divine seemed not only real but also familiar, like a foggy memory. In that instant, not only did I recognize the frightened, vulnerable, and needy child inside me—as it is inside all of us—I also forgave her. That moment was my first real experience of grace.

"STILLING" THE DESTINATION OF SPIRITUAL READING

But grace was no match for my long-engrained patterns of putting the needs of others before my own. I reconsidered my overseas sabbatical journey. Thanks to a convergence that could not have been a coincidence, however, a few months before my flight, a friend experiencing her own painful life transition posted to her social media feed a verse by Irish poet John O'Donohue. By then I was in a new home, one free of daily disrespect and worse. One morning I settled into a comfortable chair, took cleansing breaths, and recognized a divine presence, both around and inside me. I read O'Donohue's *For a New Beginning, A Blessing* poem until one passage stood out. I repeated these words to myself in silence. They not only shimmered with hope; they *shined* with grace:

> Unfurl yourself into the grace of this beginning
> That is one with your life's desire.
> Awaken your spirit to adventure;
> Hold nothing back. Learn to find ease in risk.

Next, I reflected on the poem's theme: that a new beginning can form inside us unnoticed until we are brave enough to take the first step forward toward it. I welcomed into my heart the notion that my overseas sabbatical could be one of "un-dependence," not a risk to my children but an expedition ripe with promise for all four of us.

As one expert in spiritual reading later advised me, I listened for an invitation in light of my current circumstances: "This invitation may be a summons toward a new awareness or action. We are summoned to stretch ourselves beyond our usual limits. We ask for the grace to have our hearts changed by what we have heard and to live out that change in concrete ways."

There was that word again: *grace.* I copied the poem, superimposed it over a photo of a narrow road in Ireland, and posted a printout on my home office filing cabinet. Whenever I wavered in my resolve to embark on this new beginning, I re-read and recited the words. In that way, a spiritual guide I had never met navigated me toward an intentional path, one that sent me to Ireland, the home of my forebears.

Thanks in part to that country's spotty cellular coverage, for six weeks I was free of endless emails from attorneys and toxic texts from my almost-ex. I focused only on reading, writing, and long runs through the winding lanes of the rugged Beara Peninsula. Whenever I encountered a scruffy-maned cob pony, or a brave ewe, or the ubiquitous and always friendly Border Collie, I'd snap a photo for my girls. (The four of us had once managed a similar menagerie of barn buddies on the farm I reluctantly left behind during my marital separation.) When bars of service allowed, I texted the photos to my girls. They replied with heart emojis.

Just days before my return flight to the United States, in an unexpected moment of connectivity, an alert jangled my phone. I stared in disbelief at several messages from my husband. They related, dryly, the horrific news of how, the weekend prior, he had deposited our 15-year-old at a Saturday night party hosted by strangers, no questions asked. Not until early the next morning did he see our daughter again, when she was prostrate in a hospital bed. EMTs had transported her after she drank vodka on an empty stomach to the point of becoming unresponsive. Realizing simultaneously my youngest's predicament and that her father delayed days before notifying me, I stifled the urge to keen like banshees, the mythical Irish spirits who wail to portend disaster. His last text was consistent with a pattern long familiar: he shifted blame to our daughter (and probably to me as well): "She's much wiser for the mistake she made."

I paced around the twin bed in my tiny Irish B&B room, trying to breathe, trying to think, trying to figure out what to do next. The temporary window of cellular service snapped shut after launching a nightmare for me, whose self-worth was defined by rescuing those I loved. I could not run to my child's bedside, could not lash out at her father, and could notify no one else to do all the above on my behalf. All I could do was cry, circle, and curse myself. I was suffocating.

Out the front door into what the Irish call a "soft" afternoon of misty rain, I fled, stopping only to borrow a pair of Wellies by the welcome mat. I charged through the yard, down a steep hill, and past an ancient ruin of a mill that once "fulled" local wool by beating it soft. I heard the cascade's cacophony long before I spied its frothy familiarity. Slipping up the stairs, I crossed an elevated bridge leading to a refuge, what was likely a special Celtic geography called a "thin place." Here, on an island, the boundary between corporeal and the Divine felt as narrow as a breath, as transparent as the spray moistening my cheeks and hair. I sat. Ferns and boughs embraced me, calmed me. No wonder, as O'Donohue wrote, ancient Celts revered nature as "a vision of the divine where...the thing that is the signature of your utmost uniqueness can somehow coalesce with the greater flow of spirit and nature in the world, all without your singular identity getting lost."

It turned out I was not lost. The soles of my rubber boots were grounded on wet clover, my bottom on a slatted bench, and my palms rested, face up, on my thighs. My eyelids settled shut. My breathing slowed as I focused on what I knew to be true: my darling daughter was no longer in immediate danger. I released the notion that protecting and parenting her was my responsibility alone. I forgave myself for not being there when she needed me most. As Melody Beattie writes, "We need to give ourselves some of the boundless loyalty that so many co-dependents are willing to give others. Out of high self-esteem will come true acts of kindness and charity, not selfishness."

"STILLING" THE DESTINATION OF SPIRITUAL READING

It turned out I was not lost.

When the next day I got a call through to my teenager, her version of events came as no surprise. Patterns of relationships with addicted people and other troubled souls are similar, as are the coping strategies we use to explain them away. During a period of sadness, she told me, after neither her father nor sisters came to cheer at her first-ever district cross-country championship race, she resorted to a solution long modeled by her father: drowning misery in alcohol. But unlike the addict in her life, my daughter took full responsibility for the frightening consequences.

With each breath, I imagined the river washing away successive waves of unearned anxiety. I called to mind a favorite stanza of O'Donohue's poem, by then memorized. "Soon you will be home in a new rhythm, For your soul senses the world that awaits you."

On that island, tucked inside the island of Ireland, I was *still*, for perhaps the first time in my adult life. While the river rushed by, I was stationary; but I was open to spirit and nature flowing both in me and through me. I rested, trusting my soul's new rhythm that was somehow in sync with the wisdom of the ages. I accepted grace, to me a gift unearned and valuable beyond price. On that bench, to which I return often in my imagination, I arrived at the path of awe and intentionality's rewarding destination: the place of self-knowledge, self-acceptance, and self-gift.

READ

Two poems by John O'Donohue are a good place to start. They are publicly available on the Internet after searching these titles:

- For One Who Is Exhausted, A Blessing
- For a New Beginning, A Blessing

REFLECT

Give yourself the gift of a place apart, a special location all your own in your home, your place of work or worship, or in nature. Appreciate with all your senses what makes that refuge special. Note how your body feels during every retreat so you can return, physically or only in your imagination.

RESPOND

Think of one responsibility you no longer need to manage. Let that burden fall, washing away like a leaf in a rushing river.

RECEIVE

Grace is like water, ready to flow into empty places if you stay open to its mystery. Accept grace when ready to continue along the intentional path toward self-knowledge.

STEP 1

"SHIMMERING" THE LIGHT OF SELF-KNOWLEDGE

Foundations that lasted the ages,
Then ripped apart at their roots....
There's no turning back, no last stand.
Heart and soul, one will burn.

Joy Division, "Heart & Soul"

"SHIMMERING" THE LIGHT OF SELF-KNOWLEDGE

A LIFETIME BEFORE my solo sojourn to Ireland, a trip with my then-new, later-ex-husband took on almost equal significance. As newlyweds, we drove south from Ohio to a place where he once lived. I'll never forget how after we crossed confusing cobwebs of bridges, which spanned marshes and bypassed a succession of quaint communities, I caught a first-glimpse of endless golden seagrass horizons foregrounded by prickly oyster-beds. The humid air, which seemed suspended just above our sunroof, smelled something like a salted caramel left to mold in the toe of a stored Christmas stocking. Later I learned the malodorous maelstrom was sulfur emitting from pluff mud, a native concoction created when freshwater silt floods salt marshes during changing tides, decomposing plants and animals in its path.

At the time of this, my first trip to South Carolina, I could not imagine that three daughters in the future would roll down car windows as soon as they saw the marshes, to catch a whiff of that singular stinkiness, a smell that signaled the nearness of a place we all grew to love: Fripp Island, South Carolina.

The narrator of a book set on the island, *The Prince of Tides*, explains the significance of that smell. "To describe our growing up in the Low Country of South Carolina...I would say, 'Breathe deeply,' and you would breathe and remember that smell for the rest of your life, the bold, fecund aroma of the tidal marsh, exquisite and sensual, the smell of the South in heat; a smell like new milk, semen, and spilled wine, all perfumed with seawater. My soul grazes like a lamb on the beauty of indrawn tides."

Tides author, Pat Conroy, was a favorite writer long before I married. My soul grazed on his elegiac descriptions of the marshlands even before experiencing them in person. When I did, Conroy's words decoded their mysterious beauty and inspired prayerful appreciation. The author once described writing as "the form that praying takes in me."

Adherents to the practice of Spiritual Reading believe such convergences of words, time, and place are never coincidental. In fact, the oscillations between hearts, minds, and unique life experiences are what can expand any "text"—including art, music, poetry, scripture, dreams, and even memories of lived experiences—to the level of prayer. All that is required is awareness of a phrase that beckons, comforts, or even unnerves and disturbs.

"*Lectio* calls us to awaken our bodies, minds, and hearts to the present moment, to the words of our selected passage, and to God's presence embedded within them and around us," writes sacred-reading teacher, Christine Valters Paintner. "Read slowly...until you come to a word, phrase, or section that *strikes a chord* in you," goes another of her instructions. "Be present to this inner experience without

"SHIMMERING" THE LIGHT OF SELF-KNOWLEDGE

judgment, and respond to these energetic 'shimmerings' within as an invitation into the ways God is working in our lives."

Perhaps driven by some unseen plan more than twenty years after my first view of the marshes, I decided to return to Conroy's words in Spiritual Reading. By then we owned a home on Fripp, stocked with native son Pat Conroy's many semi-autobiographical novels and DVDs of feature films based on them. One morning I pulled *The Prince of Tides* from the shelf and reclined on a chaise in our master bedroom, looking out over golden seagrass that stretched toward a distant bridge. My teens had headed for the pool, and their father was likely several holes and high balls into a golf game somewhere. That left me free to skim a familiar chapter about family vacations. "The safe places could only be visited," I read. "They could only grant a momentary intuition of sanctuary."

Connecting that text to my life was almost too easy. Only during vacations on Fripp were my daughters and I spared drink-fueled dramas with my spouse, which in Ohio and on other vacations could happen at any time. We seemed buffered by my husband's nostalgia for a place where he had partied as a Naval officer. A more likely blessing was the all-day buzz he titrated while the women of his family enjoyed more sober pursuits without him. Recognizing the truth of the next lines by Conroy, however, made me wince: "The moment always came when we had to return to our real life to face the wounds and grief indigenous to our home."

The husband/father who showed up at Fripp every other summer and many spring breaks could be as smart, as funny, and as full of potential as the man I fell in love with. Perhaps some Low Country Carolina magic cast a delusional spell making me think binges elsewhere were the exceptions, not the (obvious) rule. One glint of soft hazel in his gaze on the island erased all memory in me of how often his eyes boiled black with rage and dilated pupils at home. An incantation of ocean waves in the distance lulled me into thinking he wanted to become well and, with my help, could be. I hardly noticed how, over the years, our family's vacation destinations shrunk to only a handful of options—his favorites. That compromise seemed small price to pay for momentary joy.

Ever so slowly, I sank into a morass of rationalization, one that Shawn Burns identifies in her book *Unhealthy Helping* as "conflating love with rescue."

"The intense shared experiences of the other's struggles and disasters and the helper's rescues," she writes, "deepen the emotional connection and feelings of intimacy.... This motivates [helpers] to reduce the other's suffering (and their own) by continued helping."

Helping was my job from the first night I met a clever but inebriated redhead at a campus bar after an Ohio State football game. As a posse of his friends fetched his beers, they helped remind him of my name. A few hours into our first date, I applied for a new position, one I rarely relinquished afterwards: the designated driver. As slowly and subtlety as tides recede to reveal mud in Carolina marshes daily, my self-image as an artist, journalist, and activist washed away to leave behind only what Jung called the "Demeter," or "Mother," archetype. As both the rescuer and caretaker of my husband, and later our daughters, I was ever the heroine, at least in my own mind. As Melody Beattie puts it, "Most of us (co-dependents) aren't even aware of what we're doing.... Many of us are convinced that rescuing is a charitable deed."

Charity was taught to me as a core Christian value. Forbearance and forgiveness were synonymous, I assumed. Holding together a marriage "'for life" was the only option. So when a couple's therapist told us I was co-dependent with my alcoholic spouse, my defense was swift and indignant. "What? I'm not the one with the problem! He is!" I had managed to earn a Ph.D. after becoming a mother and maintained a successful career, first as a writer, then teaching journalism as a college professor. "How could *that* be in any way dependent?" I whined. Denial is perhaps the most effective coping strategy those in relationship with addicts can cultivate.

The term I was so offended by—*co-dependency*—first became popular in substance abuse treatment circles in the 1980s to characterize lopsided relationships consumed and controlled by one person's addiction. Experts continue to argue about the expression, which is neither a clinical diagnosis nor a personality disorder. Ann Smith, author of *Grandchildren of Alcoholics*, prefers the term "insecure attachment" to describe adults who, because of past experiences, stay in unhealthy relationships, usually out of fear: "When a person or family is dealing with an ongoing problem...they develop patterns that are an attempt to decrease anxiety and increase attachment, but that may be ineffective and make the situation worse."

Semantics aside, therapists universally agree nothing good results from unequal relationships, when one adult caregiver only gives, enabling a loved one to take, while giving little or nothing in return. As the "strong one" in a partnership, the "good" caregivers become expert at denial, unable and unwilling to acknowledge their own pain. By contrast, in healthy relationships, both parties give and receive equally most of the time, keeping their own identities separate from the other person, not "enmeshed."

There was no denying that lack of self-esteem was always part of my identity.

Though I pushed back on the label of co-dependency in public, in private there was no denying that lack of self-esteem was always part of my identity. When seeing a flawed reflection in my mirror, I often told her to be grateful for even one-sided relationships. As Melody Beattie, writer of the seminal book about co-dependency writes, "Some of us may not even be aware of our low self-esteem and self-hatred because we have been comparing ourselves to the alcoholics and other crazy people in our lives; by comparison, we come out on top."

The only place my self-questioning never trespassed was within my comfort zone of reading and writing. Long before it became Pinterest-trendy to annotate books, I unapologetically turned-down page corners, scribbled margin notes, and inserted scraps of paper filled with my own words, stopping at nothing in order to note and capture and possess all that "shimmers" in the wisdom of others. My scrivenings were part therapy and part prayer, just as they were for my favorite novelist, Pat Conroy. That is why, on one Fripp Island vacation day, I decided to visit nearby places described in his body of literature. I hoped proximity to his creativity might somehow spark a return of my own.

Before pulling my minivan from the driveway, I cued up a playlist of post-punk club jams, which were once the soundtrack of my single days. Tunes by New Order, the Clash, and Joy Division, helped me recall how long ago I had "danced like no one was watching." Pounding synths connected my heartbeat to a past pulse of life and creation, just like the "om" mantra of Eastern meditation practice does. Because music offers gifts that can fill a soul, Spiritual Reading can be practiced using songs, rhythms, and other sounds as "texts." Saint Hildegard of Bingen once wrote that "Music arouses the sluggish soul to watchfulness. It has the power to soften even hard hearts." Thanks to my Spiritual Reading practice, I always tune into music as a potential portal of wisdom, whether the song is an oldie or the latest Taylor Swift chart-topper.

That day, my softened heart began to sing, solo and a little off key for sure, as I drove across three bridges to St. Helena Island. The community was once called Frogmore by descendants of enslaved West Africans who, due to the remoteness of the sea islands, retained a distinct language, culture, and history up until present day. I learned all I knew about the Gullah people from the very first Conroy book I ever read. *The Water Is Wide* is an autobiographic novel about a white teacher who educates Gullah children on a remote South Carolina barrier island. Conroy maintained a lifelong love and respect for the people of these Low Country communities.

I, too, preferred the rumpled authenticity of Gullah islands over the pruned perfection of Fripp, a playground populated primarily by retired Midwestern snowbirds in cookie-cutter second homes. In contrast, on St. Helena, tangled wisteria crawled up signposts to unpaved roads, colorfully named for one-time residents (Clifford & Minnie, Susie, Martha, and Helen). Along State Route 21, my van passed squat, cement-block houses painted brilliant cerulean—known locally as "haint blue" and meant to ward off evil spirits. This day I was in search of spirits, but not the unsettled ones known to haunt the island's plantation-era church ruin and graveyard known as the "Church of Ease." My destination was a cemetery managed by a Black faith congregation first established in 1855 and still going strong today.

I almost missed the unmarked entrance of Memorial Gardens, where a chain-link fence surrounded a stubbed drive and handful of headstones. There weren't many parking locations within the scant acre, so I brought my car to rest under two green-scarved live oaks. It was not difficult to find the final resting place of local-son Conroy, the only grave encircled by pinecones and littered with trinkets left by visitors before me. I offered a few Hail Marys for the troubled soul who, despite literary success, spent a lifetime bathing wounds of a dysfunctional childhood with alcohol and other addictive substances. Like the soul I had married, the writer left in his wake broken families and other estranged relationships. Though I knew he was more a cultural than practicing Catholic, I hoped my prayers would bring repose to us both. In a 2009 interview, he said "I no longer believe there's any such thing as an ex-Catholic. I'm a Catholic, period.... I think I'm the kind of writer I am today, in part, because of it. And I'm still a believer. But this is a strict church. According to the laws of the Catholic Church, I will go to hell."

After finishing my silent supplications, I noticed a plastic box mounted on a stake near the marker identifying the author as "The Prince of Tides." Inside I discovered more prayers, etched on notebook paper, post-it notes, and other pulpy scraps offering personal testimonies from fellow fans of his place-based fiction. I returned to my car to fetch a journal page, figuring if prayers didn't do the job on behalf of Conroy, perhaps a pen-to-paper tribute might.

Re-reading Conroy during my morning meditation time that day sparked a notion that perhaps I would return to my own writing someday. Thinking there was no time like the present, I penned an anonymous fan letter to a dead man. "Even before I witnessed with my own eyes the marsh's raw siennas changing to ochre to burnt sienna as the sun arced an island bridge," I scribbled, "before I appreciated first-hand the transformation of a sinewy river to a flood with the changing tides, I loved this place through your words. Before I saw for myself the flash of an egret's winging across a canvas-colored background, I was invited here by your unsentimental devotion to place. Thank you." I stuffed the paper into the overflowing box, and returned to my van.

Next I visited the church Conroy once attended with his siblings and parents as a teen, the historic St. Peter's in downtown Beaufort. Again I was most attracted to the graveyard, pausing there to contemplate both Conroy's death and his unhappy life, which he resolved in his last book, a memoir. He wrote about accepting his loved ones for who they were, not who he wanted them to be, including the narcissistic father he dubbed the Great Santini, his long-suffering mother who eventually divorced her abuser, and several siblings who struggled with mental illness and lost, including one to suicide. In *The Death of Santini*, the author repeated an observation first penned in *Prince of Tides*: "In families, there are no crimes beyond forgiveness."

As a passage I once considered during Spiritual Reading, this sentenced shimmered, but the light it shed was harsh. Sometimes words encountered during the practice cause us to be unsettled, to question, and to shake our heads "no."

"As you listen for the word or phrase," writes Christine Valters Paintner, "you are opening yourself to unexplored areas that may stir difficult feelings. Most often these are the places that also need healing."

Because my husband's crimes were ongoing, forgiveness as I understood it seemed impossible. Only duty and love for my children compelled me to return to my family that day, temporarily recharged by the rarity of an independent day trip. Before leaving the church parking lot, I cued the song "Love Will Tear Us Apart" by Joy Division. Just as ancient monks often paused and pondered scripture, I remained in park and allowed the lyrics to sink into my body, mind, and heart. Metaphorically, they reflected the tenuous nature of all of our relationships. Literally they represented songwriter Ian Curtis's grief over an extra-marital affair. "Resentment rides high but emotions won't grow," the band intoned. "We're changing our ways, taking different roads."

A few months later, after I was somehow blamed for a succession of binges by my husband that imperiled my life and those of my daughters, my family arrived at a crossroads. The addict in our household wouldn't make the right turn toward AA and counseling, so I redirected instead. My route was unchartered, like those unpaved roads first glimpsed in South Carolina. I could only pray the destination was a happiness that did not depend on the happiness of others.

As Beattie writes, "To honor the self is to be in love… with our possibilities for growth and for experiencing joy, in love with the process of discovery and exploring our distinctively human potentialities."

The strains of Joy Division ended and a new song began that spring afternoon of what was, in retrospect, Spiritual Reading. I motored back across now familiar roadways and bridges to return to my family. But my cosmic course had diverged, if ever so slightly. Both shimmering on the page and in my soul was a new awareness, a friendly reminder of who I was and who I might become. I silently whispered a prayer of thanksgiving for the "texts" of that day and for the courage to begin to interpret them with new eyes.

"SHIMMERING" THE LIGHT OF SELF-KNOWLEDGE

READ

Think about times in your life when particular words or images moved you, speaking to your heart. What books, poems, songs, artworks, short stories, articles, or memories made a lasting impression on you? Seek out those texts again, this time finding new meaning that "shimmers" from a different vantage point of your current life experience and desired change of perspective.

REFLECT

If a phrase, lyric, or image in your Spiritual Reading triggers a memory of a time *before* a troubled relationship, take a moment to rest there, whether the moment makes you comfortable or uncomfortable. Consider how your self-perception is changing now.

RESPOND

If the convergence of memory and text offers a new insight into your authentic self, consider changing your priorities, even for just one day. Might you be strong, valuable, and good simply because of your humanity, not because of all you do to help others? In what tangible, immediate way might you help *yourself*?

RECEIVE

Caring souls who derive self-worth from helping addicts fall into self-defeating thoughts that therapists call mind traps, usually based on irrational beliefs. Moments of authentic self-knowledge offer opportunities to question any self-beliefs that are emotional, reactive, and overly personalized. If such insights arise during spiritual reading, accept them without judgment.

STEP 2

"SETTLING" WHEN YOU'VE DONE ALL YOU CAN

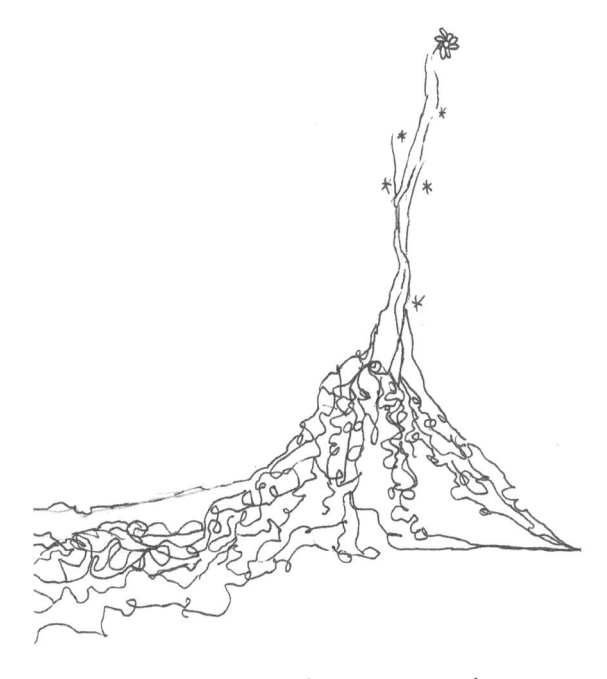

Until all that is made seems as nothing,
no soul can be at rest.
When a soul sets all at nothing for love,
to have one who is everything that is good,
then it is able to receive spiritual rest.

from *Divine Revelations of Love*

"SETTLING" WHEN YOU'VE DONE ALL YOU CAN

THE GIVEN NAME of the woman who authored the quote above in the late 14th century is not known, nor are many details of her life. Though this seminal text, a memoir about her mystical experiences, is thought to be the first book written in English by a woman, her relative obscurity is just as she wished it to be. Historians have christened her "Julian of Norwich" because for some forty years she lived in a 100-square-foot cell attached to St. Julian's church in Norwich, England. By her own will, she elected a life of solitude and contemplation as an avowed anchoress, never to leave a tiny "hold" where she experienced her glimpses of Heaven.

As early as the third century C.E., men and women retreated to hermitages when their sense of the sacredness of life ran counter to their lived experiences, when their human relationships were misused or counterproductive, and when power and material possessions became overemphasized. By leaving all worldly goods behind, these "contemplatives," as they are often called, abandoned all notions of self-importance in favor of loving only the Divine.

Ironically, perhaps, when Desert Mothers (Ammas), Fathers (Abbas), and hermits like Julian, left the world, the world was drawn to them. Spiritual travelers journeyed to monasteries, hermitages, and other remote locations to ask these wise ones for "a word." When holy men and women obliged with pithy sayings or faith-filled fables, so began the earliest practice of Spiritual Reading. While centuries later one window of Julian's room opened to the church so she could attend Mass, another opened to the outside, allowing pilgrims to seek her advice and counsel. In that way, she lived a solitary life of prayer and contemplation, enclosed and yet exposed, hidden and yet visible. She prayed for others and interceded for them with the Divine.

Soon after filing for a divorce, I inhabited an anchor-hold of sorts, but against my will. Thanks to a legal system that recognizes both parties living in a "marital home" as equals during legal separation, I could not force my husband to move out of the house deeded to my name. Self-imposed exile in what was once a shared master bedroom on the second floor of our Cape Cod seemed to be my only option as attorneys wrestled again and again to stalemate. Unlike Julian, I left my garret-like room for work and to care for my children and our farm animals, struggling all the while to remain hopeful, faithful, and sane.

As a warped version of my family's once-and-future life carried on outside my "cell," I endeavored arduously to prepare heart and mind for sessions of Spiritual Reading. Sometimes words shimmered, but I could not "settle." Unless alone, a rare occurrence, any attempt at paying sacred attention to my life was replaced by chronic, chest-tightening alertness for possible danger. While abuse by the man-of-the-house was most often verbal and psychological, that was hardly a guarantee of safety. The drive to protect our three children was so primal, so hopelessly engrained, that I constantly surveilled, eavesdropped, and hoarded any information I could glean that might fortify and shield my children and me.

To shore up my tentative grasp of sanity in an insane environment, I filled my second-floor warren with portals to my past, both objects and activities as distraction from the maelstrom of manipulation swirling on the floors beneath me. I dusted off my guitar, enrolled in an online art class, pinned every inspirational quote I could find on mirrors and Instagram, and filled bookshelves with self-help and spiritual titles promising to offer me even a whisper of wisdom and solace. So, in practice, I traded one disordered attachment for others.

The great ascetic, Julian, released herself from most material possessions. Even the modern-day spiritual teacher Bede Griffiths advises that before we attempt the disciplined practice of Spiritual Reading, we must "remove everything that prevents you from listening to God speaking in you."

Not only did my material talismans deafen me, my lifelong patterns of enabling also blinded me even as I was finding the road to healing. For years, I thought I could create the father my daughters deserved, whether that meant signing him up to coach their sports teams or forcing his participation in activities they enjoyed even if he did not. Rather than expecting to share household and parenting tasks, I felt it was best—easiest, wisest, safest—to do most things solo. Even during our co-habiting separation, I insisted on managing the unmanageable: a household occupied by an unpredictable and vindictive bully. I typed, printed, and posted parenting schedules and job assignments. When he ignored them, I internalized his neglect by revising and reprinting our assignments—which yielded the same results. What was reasonable to expect from him became so elusive that if he cooperated, even in the most insignificant way, I was fooled into thinking that I was in control, a self-soothing lie characteristic of unbalanced relationships.

"When we attempt to control people and things that we have no business controlling, we are controlled," writes Melody Beattie. "We forfeit our power to think, feel, and act in accordance with our best interests."

----- ✲

The words of Julian and other wise scribes that I discovered in my anchor-hold during Spiritual Reading were like a sacred susurration, across time and space. I inclined my ear toward a subtle energy, a synchronous vibration well below my physical hearing range, that seemed positive and challenging at the same time. Reading, mediation, and contemplation not only calmed my anxiety; I began to appreciate the daily practice of Spiritual Reading as an act of resistance. Even if I struggled to "settle" my mind and body, this defiance awakened in me an inner voice to drown out the babble of my self-judgment and resentment. I would not allow my hurt to harden my body, mind, or spirit, as it had so many troubled souls in my life. The past would not limit my future possibilities. Grace was mine, a gift opening me to advice from unexpected guides along my intentional spiritual path.

For too long, the credential letters after my professional signature limited my understanding of whom I should trust as experts on *any* topic. I snobbishly respected the advice of only advanced-degreed therapists, well-schooled theologians, and spiritual teachers endorsed by traditional institutions. Until, that is, I attended my first recovery meetings—both Al-Anon for families of alcoholics and Co-Dependent Anonymous fellowships. There I finally discovered that lived experience and sincere self-gift are better guardrails along the path toward healing than any degree or title. Former addicts and recovered co-dependents offered me sage advice, asking nothing in return. Others left behind breadcrumbs in texts suitable for Spiritual Reading, including AA's daily meditation books such as *One Day at a Time*. When self-knowledge finally yielded self-acceptance, I no longer needed the lifetime shield of self-righteousness I had fashioned for myself. I accepted roadside assistance from even the most unlikeliest of sources.

One person who helped was a long-ago friend who circled back into my orbit long enough to suggest I read a slim paperback by a Jesuit priest whose teachings were at one time censured by Catholic Church leaders suspicious of his melding of Eastern and Western moral philosophies and practices, including Buddhism and Taoism. *Awareness: The Perils and Opportunities of Reality* was a transcript of retreats given by Anthony DeMello, who died in 1987. Though DeMello's repetitive admonitions hardly made for great literature, their directness was just the kick in the pants I needed. For example, this sentence shimmered in connection to what I had learned about my past pain: "Suffering points up an area where you have not yet grown, where you need to grow and be transformed and change."

We should approach Spiritual Reading defenseless, says Cistercian monk Michael Casey in his book *Strangers to the City*, because the gift of salvation very often runs counter to our expectations. "We open ourselves to the text. We approach it in a spirit of faith and obedience, ready to perceive in what we read the word of God, the will of God, the action of God coming to save us.... We approach our reading as a disciple comes to a master: receptive, docile, willing to be changed."

I was changed by DeMello chapters such as "Permanent Worth," "Addictive Love," and, most of all,

"Detachment," a concept new to me. "Someone brainwashed me into thinking I need his or her love," DeMello explained, "but I really don't. I don't need anybody's love. I just need to get in touch with reality. Reality is that eternal life is now...[but] we have no notion about it at all. We are too distracted with this attachment."

While these words seemed to contradict what I had been taught about Christian love, I discovered that many great spiritual thinkers taught that holding on desperately to anything in this world diminished our ability to love completely and grow spiritually. Julian knew that. So did Meister Eckhart, a medieval German mystic whose teachings about detachment as a first step toward the Divine were once condemned and suppressed. Eckhart is now revered by a variety of seekers, including Zen Buddhists, Sufi Muslims, Advaita Vedanta Hindus, Jewish Kabbalists, and even those considering themselves "spiritual but not religious."

One of Oprah Winfrey's self-help gurus, Eckhart Tolle, actually changed his first name as homage to this revered philosopher. "A detached heart desires nothing at all, nor has it anything it wants to get rid of," Meister Eckhart taught. "Therefore, it is free of all prayers, or its prayer consists of nothing but being uniform with God."

Authentic spiritual growth requires setting aside the urge to "do something." When we are enmeshed too tightly in the lives of those who need help, it is tempting to expect a higher power to intervene, but it is not logical to expect such intervention in exchange for virtuous self-martyrdom or scrupulous spiritual practices. Even our making extreme sacrifices offers only an illusion of control.

According to DeMello, detachment requires total surrender. "You don't need pushing. You don't need effort.... Slow down and taste and smell and hear, and let your senses come alive. If you want a royal road to mysticism, sit down quietly and listen to all the sounds around you. You do not focus on any one sound; you try to hear them all. Oh, you'll see the miracles that happen to you when your senses come unclogged."

I began to see the gifts of my place apart in our house.

With DeMello's guidance, I began to see the gifts of my place apart in our house. Only after detaching from my family's usual patterns did I begin to see the unhealthy compromises I had made unwittingly. Perched above my husband's gaslighting, it no longer confused me. His insults of "you're crazy," no longer rang true. I gave up my self-appointed job as a human shield, knowing that even my daughters had important lessons to learn from experiencing the full measure of their father's manipulation. Ironically, I was liberated more than ever by that list of shared tasks that he ignored, because the responsibilities were distributed equally for the first time in our marriage, and it was obvious—at least to me—who was doing what they had agreed to do and who was not. Like Julian, I found liberation in my little cell on the top floor because it provided both perspective and an opportunity to seek holiness (or wholeness) for myself alone.

But even holiness proved inadequate armor for war with an evil that intensified the longer I stayed in the house. My husband's unprovoked verbal abuse of our daughters worsened until they begged him to move out. When that didn't work, the building toxicity found me as a target. While driving home from work one day, the notion of sending the car off the road "to show them how much they'd miss me" passed like a dark shadow across my consciousness. I knew then what I must do. As Melody Beattie observes, "for each of us there comes a time to let go. You will know when that time comes. When you have done all that you can do, it is time to detach."

I traded my anchor-hold for a four-bedroom rental home in a nearby town, sure my daughters would follow. That they did not, choosing instead to remain in their childhood home, was both painful and unsettling to me. One daughter never slept in the room I made for her; another lived with me for only a short time; and another split time between her parents until announcing that the expensive condo where her actively alcoholic father then lived with his new girlfriend felt "more like home."

No matter how tightly my ego clung to the notion I must save my daughters, I came to a realization that young adults who saw no need to be rescued could not be rescued. Because my girls had access to both cars and choices, I was usually alone in my new home. One morning soon after my move, I sat in what was once lawn furniture, now inside my home office. As I imagine happened often with Julian, solitude became a portal to prayer. After just a few deep breaths, I settled. A deep meditative state came over me, unaided by any reading, praying, or begging for divine grace. When I returned to attention from my reveries, I felt restored. Detachment was not only possible; I suddenly understood, it offered much-needed gifts.

Successful detachment from the dysfunctional relationship with my husband eventually made it easier to let go of others—with a co-worker, a sibling, and other kin. I found that detachment is often the most loving forgiveness possible we can offer. When I walked away from troubled relationships, I liberated everyone from the need to keep up appearances. I spared loved ones from what I now recognize as my unsolicited advice and well-meaning attempts to control their choices. Taking a cue from Julian, I interceded for them instead, but not by making promises or doing ascetic practices. The scriptures describe "intercessory prayer" as a means of helping souls unable to help themselves, those unwilling or ill-equipped to seek divine assistance directly. Catholics often invoke the help of saints, like Saint Raphael, for this task. During the response stage of one Spiritual Reading session, I composed my own surrendering supplication, offered on behalf of lost loved ones, including my daughters:

> Dear God, please walk with my dear ones because I cannot. Straighten their paths even as they diverge from mine. In *your* love, let them know *my* love. In your endless mercy, help them understand the best forgiveness I can offer is this: to accept their choices and show enough respect for their journey that I step out of the way.

"When I die to the need for people," DeMello wrote, "then I am right in the desert. In the beginning it feels awful, it feels lonely, but if you can take it for a while you're suddenly discovering that it isn't lonely at all. It is solitude, it is aloneness, and the desert begins to flower."

READ

Adopt an attitude of openness to all writings that might offer you insight, especially those suggested by wise friends. Experiment with these suggestions, but be willing to move beyond anything that does not in the moment "shimmer" for you right then. It is always possible to return to a text later, when the timing is right.

REFLECT

Accept and believe that along the intentional path of Spiritual Reading, you alone are the best judge of what your soul needs, what leads you to self-knowledge and self-acceptance. Be wary of guides offering simple answers, the wrong kind of "settling."

RESPOND

Try loving detachment from anything you are clinging to: a person, a material object, a place, a self-image, a hope, even a book or poem or piece of music. Letting go of even the smallest desires builds your capacity to release from them more easily in the future.

RECEIVE

Some practitioners call the final stages of Spiritual Reading "repose," a time when we rest in the Divine. Be aware of unconditional love speaking to your deepest being, such as in a deep breath or a fluttering heart. Trust the answers you find there.

STEP 3

"SAVORING" THE HOSPITALITY OF JOY

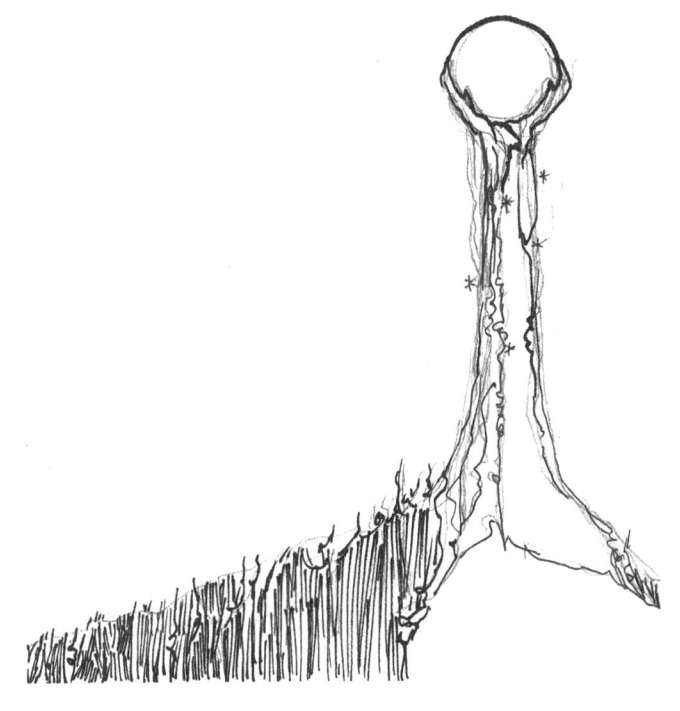

The most visible joy can only reveal itself to us
when we've transformed it, within.

Rainer Maria Rilke

"SAVORING" THE HOSPITALITY OF JOY

INTERNALIZING THE gifts of sacred texts has been the goal of many spiritual seekers across the centuries. Desert mothers, fathers, and monastics of all faiths often meditated on just one line of holy wisdom for weeks at a time. They repeated, recited, connected, collated, mixed, and marinated words into a daily stew of prayer and work (in Latin *Ora et Labora*), until deeper meaning soaked, soused, and steeped into every part of their body, heart, and soul. They committed the words to memory. Such "savoring" begins the meditation stage of Spiritual Reading. In that way—from within—words allow us to experience not transitory happiness, but transformative joy.

Memorization as a learning strategy fell out of favor decades ago, but thankfully not before I was required to recite a poem in front of my second-grade classmates. Reading and repeating the words of Robert Louis Stevenson sealed them forever in my hippocampus, a snippet of childhood joy I had no trouble sharing with my young daughters decades later as we sailed toward cirrus clouds on backyard swings each spring:

> How do you like to go up in a swing,
> Up in the air so blue?
> Oh, I do think it the pleasantest thing
> Ever a child can do!

Those words triggered a visual memory, too, of sweet illustrations by Hilda Boswell in my personal copy of *A Child's Garden of Verses*. Thanks to the miracle of the Internet, I confirmed that, yes, little girls on swings once wore dresses, knee socks, and patent leather shoes.

Also tucked away in my memory is a mélange of mnemonic devices, song lyrics, limericks, and aphorisms—many of questionable utility—along with prayers "learned by heart" as a child and as an adult. While it is tempting to discount the value of traditional spoken prayers, especially with all those *thee's* and *thou's*, I often return to these memorized words with intention. Precisely because these ancient rhythms have become part of my body and mind, I can now recite them slowly, meditatively, with little risk of forgetting the next line.

I can savor them.

According to a recent scientific study about savoring, the capacity to "attend to, appreciate, and enhance the positive experiences in one's life" is associated with benefits ranging from greater self-esteem to increased happiness. The study categorized both reactive and proactive savoring, finding a distinct difference between genders in their ability to savor: Women are better "savor-ers" and are also more likely than men "to share their joyful sentiments with others...reflect on their good fortune and avoid negative thoughts that hinder savoring." On my social feeds, those most likely to post inspirational quote memes are undoubtedly female.

While the study explained the benefits of seeing the world through rose-colored glasses, it failed to address the risks of life as a perpetual Pollyanna. In my darkest moments enmeshed with the troubled souls of others, including my former spouse, I relied heavily on gratitude lists, pinning one shiny moment together with what I thought I wanted and needed. I crafted a crazy quilt of love and longing, but one never adequate to warm a family that contained an active addict. Even after detaching from this, my most dependent relationship, the impulse to stitch, patch, and repair happiness was driven by the delusion that what I had was both the best I could hope for and all that I deserved.

Successful savoring requires more than gratitude. If a social media algorithm can recognize a happy photo and feed it back to us as a positive memory, joy in our personal life must instead require something deeper and lasting. Spiritual writer Henri Nouwen defined joy as the "fruit of hope," which "frees us from the need to predict the future and allows us to live in the present with deep trust." Defined this way, genuine joy is the antidote for the persistent anxiety suffered by those in dysfunctional relationships.

"When I trust deeply that today God is truly with me and holds me safe in a divine embrace, guiding every one of my steps," Nouwen wrote in *Here and Now*, "I can let go of my anxious need to know how tomorrow will look or what will happen next month or next year. I can be fully where I am and pay attention to the many signs of God's love within me and around me."

According to ancient and modern thinkers alike, savoring requires a loving detachment from oneself, cultivating a kind and accepting "internal witness." In Hindu philosophy, one strives to develop *Sakshi*, a "pure awareness" beyond time and space, a triad involving the experiencer, the experiencing, and what is experienced. *Sakshi* witnesses all thoughts, words, and deeds without interfering with them or being affected by them.

The twentieth-century monk Thomas Merton drew from Islamic mysticism when he wrote that the "virgin point" of the soul—the part of ourselves untouched by our daily fears and anxieties—is where the Divine dwells. "At the center of our being is a point of nothingness which is untouched by sin and illusion," Merton wrote in *Conjectures of a Guilty Bystander*, "a point of pure truth, a point or spark which belongs entirely to God.... It is in everybody." Sufis believe the hospitality of this "point of nothingness" is accessible only to a higher power.

Circa 529-530, Benedict of Nursia wrote a "rule of life" admonishing the Christian faithful to welcome any stranger as Christ. Then and now, Benedictines living both within and outside of monasteries apply that hospitality to contemplative reading. When "strangers"—a word that connotes the full spectrum of human emotions—knock at our inner door, they too must be welcomed and recognized as bearers of wisdom. Accepting thoughts with a benign wonder and curiosity allows practitioners of Spiritual Reading to attend to an inner voice that is not judgmental.

In this way, all connections, feelings, and memories—even confusing or painful ones—can be processed. Buddhist monk Thich Nhat Hanh explains that the interior witness is, above all, compassionate: "The Buddhist attitude is to take care of anger. We don't suppress it. We don't run away from it. We just breathe and hold our anger in our arms with utmost tenderness. Becoming angry at your anger only doubles it and makes you suffer more."

Therapists agree, warning that deeply empathetic people with insecure attachments become more adept at managing the emotions of others than they do acknowledging their own. As a well-tuned barometer, for example, I routinely warned my children to shelter in their rooms any time an offhanded comment threatened to alert, hurt, or upset their father. In that way, responsibility for his feelings became theirs and mine, not his. Once, a marriage therapist asked my former spouse to name just one emotion he had experienced that day. He stared into space and could not answer until, of course, I answered for him, as the therapist was quick to point out.

Feeling the feelings of others, while suppressing our own, can seem a form of kindness, an empathetic way of loving another person, but doing so comes with painful and lasting physical, emotional, and spiritual consequences to ourselves and others.

Emotions are our body's early warning indicators and motivators, sometimes signaling danger and the need for action. Only after years of therapy did I realize I had been raised—by a very religious but co-dependent family—to minimize my feelings as less important than the feelings of others. The hidden message of my all my gratitude lists I wrote then was that I "shouldn't feel" sad or angry or deprived. The lists were really a futile means of self-scolding, a stubborn penance for my inability to spin, single-handedly, the dross of incredibly happy moments—the first laugh of a baby daughter, the sweetness of the lilacs in the yard, the beauty of my family in church at Christmas—into lasting and joyous gold.

Counselor Scott Egleston, co-author of *The Language of Letting Go*, describes how, over time, those in relationships with addicts feel unworthy of happiness to the point of self-sabotage. We become suspicious of contentment because another crisis is always just around the corner. If not, we seek it out or create conflict. Even years after escaping from active addicts in my life, I'd catch myself doom-scrolling social media any time life seemed too good to be true. And worst of all, when I wasn't wallowing in a pit of disaster-thinking and conflicting emotions—both mine and those of others—I actually felt nothing at all.

"The big reason for not repressing feelings is that emotional withdrawal causes us to lose our positive feelings," writes Melody Beattie in *Codependent No More*. My own recovery required finding a calm core of compassion for myself, a kindly interior witness. Only then would I experience true happiness.

Fortunately for me, I rediscovered the essays of Oregon-based Catholic writer Brian Doyle as texts I could savor during my Spiritual Reading. Doyle first gained national attention—and mine—with the essay "Leap," published just after 9/11. Remarkably, in that darkest of tragedies, the author magically manifested hope and joy. "A couple leaped from the south tower, hand in hand. They reached for each other and their hands met and they jumped…. A fireman was killed by a person falling from the sky. But a man reached for a woman's hand and she reached for his hand and they leaped out the window holding hands…. It is the most powerful prayer I can imagine, the most eloquent, the most graceful…. It is what makes me believe that we are not craven fools and charlatans to believe in God, to believe that human beings have greatness and holiness within them."

Doyle witnessed and wrote about the holiness in the commonplace. Once, after documenting an entire day observing people who held hands, he concluded, "It turned out to be one of the most amazing days there ever was." In the ordinary moment of one boy running with his brother to catch a school bus, he saw "a glint of mad love for his brother in his face, a kind of shining thing, some kind of absolute joy just that they were holding hands.... That stays with me. That kid was thrilled to have a hand in his hand, and really, when you think about it, what could be cooler than that?"

Doyle called himself "The Story Catcher," one who used narrative to capture and reveal the complexity of human happiness: tragedies revealing truth, grief yielding gratitude, and poignancy arising from pain. He never resorted to bland bromides or pin-able platitudes. When I read his stories with intention, words to ponder not only shimmered—they illuminated. Doyle was for me "The Joy Catcher."

When I discovered a prayer he wrote after he was diagnosed with the brain tumor that ended his life on Earth too young in 2017, the words seemed to hoist me from shifting sands of suffering to solid ground. "I close my eyes and weep with joy that I was alive," Doyle's *Last Prayer* concluded, "and blessed beyond measure, and might well be headed back home to the incomprehensible Love from which I came." The author's confidence that infinite love was possible, his interior witness that he shared with the world, awakened my own.

"SAVORING" THE HOSPITALITY OF JOY

Once I set aside my dysfunctional "gratitude lists" and sought professional help to process my emotions, lasting joy seemed within my reach. No one can make us feel a certain way or can change how we feel unless we give him or her the power to do so. One therapist provided this metaphor for healthy empathy: If loved ones are lost in a pit of sadness, I can join them, but only long enough to show them the way out. I must immediately climb the ladder back to ground level, offering them assistance only in the form of witness, example, and prayer.

Once I sought professional help, lasting joy seemed within my reach.

Spiritual Reading was a ladder out of that pit, offering reconnection to my emotions through savoring. When I learned that information is better stored in memory if, at the moment of reading, one breathes in through the nose, I sometimes "inhaled" wise words just as I might savor a favorite food or flower by first breathing in its smell. Connecting senses in this way enhances meditation. "The soul vivifies the body and conveys the breath of life to the senses; the body draws the soul to itself and opens the senses; and the senses touch the soul and draw the body," wrote Hildegard of Bingen, the medieval mystic, gifted healer, and expert practitioner of inner hospitality as a pathway to joy.

The trinity of soul, sense, and body still vivifies for me the ending verses of Robert Louis Stevenson's poem. My mind's eye conjures the illustration of a knee-socked girl kicking off Mary Janes at the pinnacle of her ascent as clearly as I see in memory my curly-headed daughters gleefully pumping their legs to go higher. My laughter and their giggles sometimes even return in the whisper of a spring breeze that I breathe in and savor. Then I am transported, higher and higher, by joy:

> Up in the air and over the wall
> Till I can see so wide...
> Up in the air I go flying again,
> Up in the air and down!

READ

Before reading, first take several slow, deep breaths in through your nose and out of your mouth. With each exhale, release all personal expectations or judgments. After reading through the selection once, choose just a few words to memorize. Repeat them until they belong to you.

REFLECT

Continue to breathe with intention as you memorize. Allow each inhale to create inner space for your intuition and imagination. Approach any images, memories, or thoughts that rise up with benign curiosity. Don't analyze; simply accept.

RESPOND

Do not judge the fears, feelings, or confusion that arise during Spiritual Reading. Learning to savor takes patience and time. Stay open to the full spectrum of possibility within your soul.

RECEIVE

This prayer of self-acceptance comes from a 12-step program of recovery from co-dependency:

> In this moment,
> I am willing to see myself as I truly am:
> a growing, unfolding, spiritual being,
> resting in the hands of a loving God.

STEP 4

"STIRRING"
A DEEPER EXPERIENCE

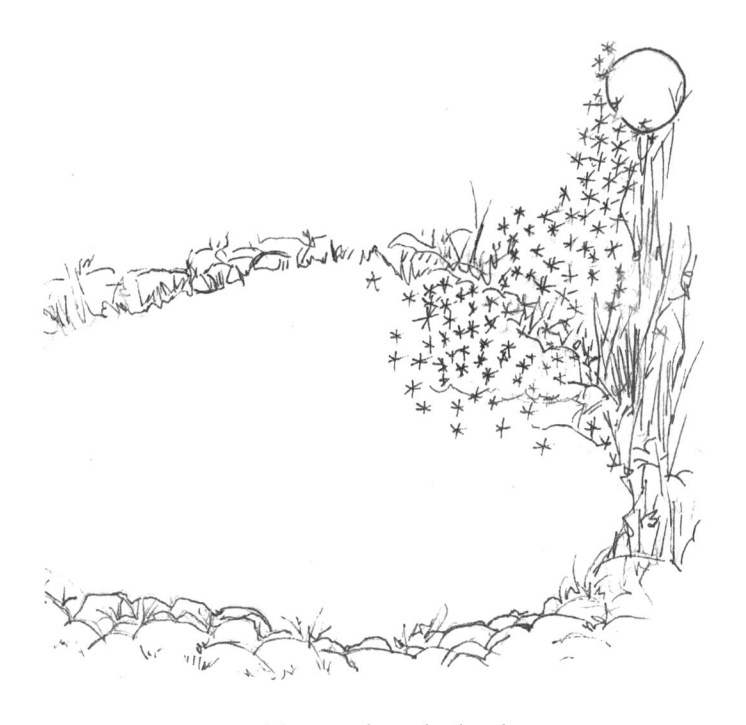

How like a widow she has become,
she that was great among the nations!
She that was a princess among the provinces
has become a vassal...
all her friends have dealt treacherously with her,
they have become her enemies.

Book of Lamentations 1:1-3

"STIRRING" A DEEPER EXPERIENCE

TEN MONTHS after filing for divorce, my fragile mental state left me no choice but to detach from a beautiful home, pets and farm animals, and the three humans I loved more than anyone else in the world, my daughters. I signed a lease on a house in a nearby city and filled it, over many weeks, with essentials stashed into my car in the early morning hours, lest their absence be noticed. I chose to leave in secret, for both my safety and that of my daughters. When it was necessary to dispatch a moving van for the only furniture not disputed as mine, the remains of my former life were packed in just two hours before anyone returned to discover my exit. Like Judah in the quote from Lamentations above, I was defeated, alone and adrift in exile.

In my new home, on the rare occasion I could settle long enough to read with intention, I gravitated toward texts that echoed my disappointment and confusion. On page 79 of a book titled *Thoughts in Solitude,* a modern-day hermit offered this humble prayer, which seemed to legitimize my state of unknowing:

> My Lord God,
> I have no idea where I am going.
> I do not see the road ahead of me.
> I cannot know for certain where it will end.

I felt compelled to learn more about the man who wrote those words, Thomas Merton, by visiting where he once lived. In retrospect, it seems irrational that I hoped a solution for my abject loneliness was a multi-day visit to a monastery where, like the monks, I would remain silent. Or maybe for the first time in my life I had nothing left to lose, nowhere else to be, and no one to answer to.

To prepare for my first Christmas alone in almost thirty years, I prayed with Cistercian monks seven times a day, beginning before dawn and ending just after dusk. For four days. the only words from my mouth were chants joining those of white-robed men at the Abbey of Gethsemani, south of Louisville. In a sparsely-adorned church, I recited the soulful stanzas of brutally beautiful poetry from the Psalms, part of Christian prayer practice called the Liturgy of the Hours. This abbey used *The Grail Psalms*, translated in the 1960s and unchanged since, perhaps because the version captures best the original rhythmic patterns of the language, what the editors call a "singing version." I was entranced not by melody, but rather the guttural emotions evoked by phrases such as "my groans," and "anguish," alongside the psalmist's assurances that "the way of the wicked leads to doom." I even purchased from the retreat center's bookstore my own copy of this version of 150 Old Testament poems. Practitioners of Spiritual Reading who favor scriptural texts for meditation and contemplation often seek out varied translations because they breathe new meaning into once-familiar passages with new syntax and vocabulary.

"STIRRING" A DEEPER EXPERIENCE

This translation of the Psalms, sometimes called The "Gelineau" Psalms after one of its translators, remains my favorite because it manages to capture a symmetry of form and feeling using words that shout at each other, clash, and cycle as human emotions do, often simultaneously: ecstatic joy partnered with lament, deep suffering alongside gratitude, and apology paired with vitriolic vengeance. The stanzas I later learned are called the "cursing Psalms" seemed then to enter my ears and travel to the sorest spots in my soul. Narrators in these verses begged deliverance from evil-doers and oppressors not unlike those in my life. Never before had biblical words called to me so clearly, like a cocktail-party effect across the centuries. The words stirred anger, but also a loving trust in cosmic justice like that promised by Gelineau's Psalm 108 (109 in other translations):

> They speak to me with lying tongues;
> they beset me with words of hate and
> attack me without cause....
> When he is judged let him come out condemned;
> Let his prayer be considered as sin.
> Psalm 108:3, 6-7

From then on, anonymous ancient psalmists have been my most reliable cosmic literary companions, willing to sit alongside my interior witness even when she feels vengeful, petty, and angry.

During Spiritual Reading, what stirs us is not always generous nor pleasant. In his book *The Prophetic Imagination*, theologian Walter Brueggemann says spiritual growth requires us to let loose cries long stuck in our throats. These are "the most visceral announcement that things are not right," he writes, "a first step toward a new consciousness."

Or, as Naomi Shihab Nye writes in her poem, *Kindness:*

> Before you know kindness as the deepest thing inside,
> you must know sorrow as the other deepest thing.
> You must wake up with sorrow.

I woke up with another emotion, too. Despite physical freedom from the slow-boil of hostility in one home, anger was my bedfellow in a new one, a spiritual stowaway that arrived in the moving van of material possessions. Therapists warn that anger and resentment take years to subside even after leaving destructive relationships or when addicts begin recovery. That's because there is power and control in unresolved anger, an effective weapon sharpened during both retreat and attack.

Therapist Melody Beattie, when in the throes of co-dependency herself, was described by a friend as "rigid and mistrustful...a self-righteous witch." Beattie writes that "if we are involved with an alcoholic, an addict, or someone with a serious ongoing problem, anger...can become our lives. The alcoholic is mad, we're mad, the kids are mad, and so is the dog.... The anger sometimes explodes like a bomb, but nobody ever gets done with it."

In unhealthy, unbalanced relationships, unresolved anger also goes underground, disguised as intimidation, control, and/or emotional manipulation. Anger is simmering just below the surface of every stare down and silent treatment, every attempt to embarrass or pressure a loved one in public, every empty threat of leaving or doing self-harm, all tactics used against me by addicts in my life.

In my family, underground rage forged a double-edged sword: one blade cruelty, the other mockery disguised as "good-natured teasing." Battles arose from a pitch of peevishness, a constant state of annoyance that therapists recognize as a characteristic of depression. Any unlucky soul might be singled out for mobbing if a powerplay opportunity arose. When the victim attempted deflection or defense, all would attack, delivering the fatal blow of "you can't take a joke." Self-preservation required participation in this bullying behavior, the only effective defense being offense. Out of necessity, I learned the best parry for put-downs was an even sharper retort.

Anger, along with anxiety, is at the center of a model psychologist Stephen Karpman developed fifty years ago called the "drama triangle." The diagram has been used to characterize disordered relationships of all kinds—with addicts, narcissists, and other manipulators who shape-shift between the roles of persecutor, victim, and rescuer as suits their self-centered needs of any moment. If an addict goes on the attack, loved ones react as victims, but only until the addict uses and requires rescue. Trapped on an always lopsided merry-go-round, those of us enmeshed with troubled souls are sentenced to a lifetime of careening from apex to apex, both stirring up and suppressing anger as we go.

There is only one escape from a drama triangle, experts say: getting off the ride.

Despite my dismount, however, I was still going in circles. After the success of past expeditions, such as that to Merton's monastery, I hoped travel would straighten my life's trajectory. Not unlike ancient pilgrims who journeyed to holy places to search for renewed faith and nearness to God, I hoped the very act of movement would yield meaning. I told myself I was not running away so much as seeking something to run towards, trusting a higher power to plan my itinerary for a few days at a time.

First, I drove south to Milledgeville, Georgia, and visited the Sacred Heart Catholic Church in the center of the small town. There my favorite author of deep faith, Flannery O'Connor, knelt every morning when able, in the fifth pew from the front on the right, saying her favorite prayer to an angel whose name in Hebrew means "God heals"—Raphael. The acclaimed master of the Southern gothic literary style suffered near-constant physical pain from lupus, a disease that claimed her father's life when she was sixteen and her own life at thirty-nine. Entering her pew, I knelt, crossed myself, then echoed words she prayed, which juxtapose what seem contrary requests: deliverance from and acceptance of pain:

> O Raphael...
> Lonely and tired, crushed by the separations
> and sorrows of life,
> we feel the need of calling you
> and of pleading for the protection of your wings,
> so that we may not be as strangers in the province of joy,
> all ignorant of the concerns of our country.

I next visited O'Connor's personal province, her family's farm, now a museum. In the bedroom where she penned two dozen short stories and two novels, despite an illness that crippled her arms and legs, the power of her perseverance was almost palpable. O'Connor, like mystics, martyrs, and spiritual seekers before her, recognized pain as a portal to greater strength.

Saint Paul once wrote that "a thorn in the flesh was given to me...to keep me from being too elated (2 Corinthians 12:7). Theologians still speculate about whether this early follower of Christ experienced a physical impairment or a spiritual one—or both. That seems a minor concern, however, given this lesson the epistolarian left behind: "...for whenever I am weak, then I am strong" (2 Corinthians 12:10).

Meditating on O'Connor's essays during my Spiritual Reading stirred realization of another apparent contradiction: during the breakup of my family, tragedies in my personal life were paired with triumphs in my professional life. My journalistic career re-ignited, offering frequent travel for freelance assignments and the thrill of essays being readily accepted and published.

Founder of the Center for Contemplation and Action, Richard Rohr, describes how paradox reveals universal truth in an essay titled "Great Love, Great Suffering": "Any journey of great love or great suffering makes us go deeper into...what can only be called universal truth. Love and suffering are finally the same."

During Rohr's own pilgrimage to Thomas Merton's hermitage at Gethsemani, he experienced this co-existence of hurt and happiness, as the "gift of tears":

> I wondered what [my] tears meant. What was I crying for? I wasn't consciously sad or consciously happy. I noticed at that moment that behind it all there was a joy, deeper than any private joy.... At

"STIRRING" A DEEPER EXPERIENCE

the same moment, I experienced exactly the opposite emotion. The tears were at the same time tears of an immense sadness—a sadness at what we're doing to the Earth, sadness about the people whom I had hurt in my life, and a sadness too at my own mixed motives and selfishness. I hadn't known that two such contrary feelings could coexist. I was truly experiencing the non-dual mind of contemplation.

What is sometimes called "coexistence of the contrary" exists not only in human experience, but in all aspects of nature. Victorian-era poet Gerard Manley Hopkins, a Catholic priest, rebelled against the rigidity of his age when he offered praise for the disorderly: the simultaneous pairing of light and dark in "dappled things." This juxtaposition in his poem *Pied Beauty* was to Hopkins testimony of God's perfect unity:

> Glory be to God for dappled things—
> For skies of couple-colour as a brinded cow;
> For rose-moles all in stipple upon trout that swim;
> Fresh-fire coal chestnut-falls; finches' wings;
> Landscape plotted and pieced—fold, fallow, and plough;
> And all trades, their gear and tackle and trim.
> All things counter, original, spare, strange;
> Whatever is fickle, freckled (who knows how?)
> With swift, slow; sweet, sour; adazzle, dim;
> He fathers-forth whose beauty is past change: Praise Him.

In her study of Black spirituality and mysticism, theologian Barbara Holmes concludes that mixed moments are to be expected—and honored—along life's path. "We are not headed toward a single goal: we are on a pilgrimage toward the center of our hearts. It is in this place of prayerful repose that joy unspeakable erupts." She describes in free verse this odd coupling of suffering and salutation:

> Joy Unspeakable
> erupts when you least expect it,
> when the burden is greatest,
> when the hope is gone
> after bullets fly.
> It rises
> on the crest of impossibility,
> it sways to the rhythm
> of steadfast hearts,
> and celebrates
> what we cannot see.

Once, another writer experienced such simultaneous brokenness and brilliance while on a walk near his home in Waltham, Massachusetts. In a moment of personal desolation, Pulitzer-Prize-winning poet Franz Wright felt a long poem "appeared" to him through what he called divine intervention. "I know for a fact that I am not intelligent enough to have written that poem with my will and my intellect," he said in a 2001 *New Yorker* interview. "Some other thing had to have entered into the process and told me what to say." That decided it: my next pilgrimage would retrace the poet's steps to the location of his creative epiphany, Purgatory Cove, somewhere along the Charles River.

A variety of Christian and rabbinical Jewish denominations imagine purgatory as a place where, after death, souls are purified by a "cleansing fire." In non-theological use, the word describes any place or condition of temporary torment. I often chose "purgatory" to describe my liminal location during a years-long bitter divorce battle: somewhere between liberty and imprisonment. In my purgatory, even minor defeats or slight disappointments could send me spiraling toward a personal Gehenna, afire with anger, resentment, and self-pity. Wright, who converted to Catholicism once he recovered from alcoholism and mental illness, described the rare moments of health before full recovery as "skeptical raptures" because he felt "at any moment I might be pulled back into that hell."

In hopes my torment would be temporary, this time I drove east from Ohio with my two youngest daughters to where Wright was inspired to write his poem, *Thanks Prayer at the Cove*. It begins:

> A year ago today
> I was unable to speak
> one syntactically coherent
> thought let alone write it down: today
> in this dear and absurdly allegorical place
> by your grace
> I am here
> and not in that graveyard, its skyline
> visible now from the November leaflessness.

Wright shared in interviews that the inspiration for this verse was an unidentified location in Waltham. With only details of the poem to guide me, I left my teens to enjoy their own adventures in Boston and struck out to find Purgatory Cove—the actual location, which was not listed on any map I could find at the time. Alternatively walking and driving, I located the cemetery the poet references in the poem, pausing there to consider my mortality, as Wright did.

But soon after, a series of misdirections and dead-ends frustrated my search. The map app on my phone was no help, registering not a single body of water that jibed even remotely with the poem's setting. At one point, I turned down a narrow street between two inlets, one green with lily pads on the right, the other stagnant with brown moss. When I ended up in a neighborhood of large homes, I backtracked a bit and parked. Discouraged, I walked toward the sepia side of the road and perched on a log perilously close both to cars whizzing by and the edge of the putrid pond. My plan was to regroup before returning to the city in defeat.

A single swan on the dark water caught my attention, stretching his neck to full length and half-raising his wings in warning. Mute swans are an unusual sight in my hometown. Every time my young daughters and I spotted such an errant migrant to Ohio, we made regular pilgrimages to the water to marvel at their grace and rarity. I recognized the swan's busking—a defensive behavior territorial males perform to protect mates and offspring. Sure enough, when the male swan, called a "cob," finally dropped his wings and relaxed, he revealed a slender pen and single cygnet in his safe shadow—his wife and child

My children were raised reading *The Ugly Duckling* and E.B. White's *Trumpet of the Swan*, learning early that swan families stick together, the parents mating for life. That memory stirred unexpected tears and, simultaneously, two very different revelations: one, my broken family paled in comparison to this swan's and, two, I had in fact arrived at my intended destination. Wright's poem about a place named Purgatory Cove featured a swan:

> the single
> dispirited swan out on the windless brown
> transparent floor floating
> gradually backward
> blackward

> no this is what I still
> can see, white
> as a joint in a box of little cigars— and where is the mate

Swans often stay on the same body of water, alone, after losing partners to illness or predation. They seem to grieve. Earlier that day, when meditating on the poem during Spiritual Reading, I had imagined Wright's swan to be a female, who, after staying loyal too long, floated backward into uncoupled loneliness. I experienced Rohr's "non-dual heart of contemplation" when I realized this: my heart—though broken, traumatized, and weary—would not, like the pen, mourn its losses forever. I was just beginning a new relationship, cautious but hopeful that the passion I found could vanquish the conquest I had suffered.

I have always loved Irish poet W.B. Yeats's elegy to the mystery and fidelity of swan couples. In "The Wild Swans at Coole," he wrote:

> Unwearied still, lover by lover,
> They paddle in the cold
> Companionable streams or climb the air;
> Their hearts have not grown old;
> Passion or conquest, wander where they will,
> Attend upon them still.

"STIRRING" A DEEPER EXPERIENCE

As I watched, the cob at Purgatory Cove glided alongside his wife, treading water to stay a single wingspan's distance. I was reminded of the couples I had observed paddling near each other in individual kayaks on the Charles River in Boston. I was long envious of such confident partnering, especially mates in church who stood so near each other that the hair on their arms touched. I was even more desirous of a love combined with shared faith, seen in couples who held hands as they knelt and prayed. My first husband had always kept physically distant from me, and likewise avoided the religious faith his daughters and I practiced fervently.

When the curious swan-child paddled nearer my seat on the shoreline, the pen snorted. Her offspring obeyed, turning tail feather and returning to the protection of the mother's pinions, all the while whistling and chirping contentedly. I smiled, recognizing in that casual conversation between mother and child swans the pattern of comfortable chatting I once shared with my daughters. During the long car ride to Boston, an enticing echo of that returned, if only temporarily.

I smiled, recognizing in that casual conversation between mother and child swans the pattern of comfortable chatting I once shared with my daughters.

My momentary reverie was replaced with the responsibility of returning to my own offspring. As I stood to bid farewell both to the foul and to at least some of the frustration I had brought with me to Purgatory Cove, I prayed my own purgatory might become a place of healing. Or at the very least, as Wright concluded in his "thanks prayer," I hoped the pairing of suffering and joy I experienced on my pilgrimage would stir an awareness that a Loving Protector is always with me:

> I didn't know you were there, God
> (that's what we call you, grunt grunt)
> as you are at every moment
> everywhere of what we call
> the future and the past.

READ

Because figurative language is open to interpretation and connection with personal experience, poetry is a good choice for Spiritual Reading. In your meditative time, ponder the verses here or, better yet, find others that "shimmer" for you.

REFLECT

Think for a moment how some of your past suffering did co-exist with joy.

RESPOND

Celebrate something that at first you did not see, perhaps writing in your journal about the co-existence of light and darkness in that moment. Recognizing such "pied beauty," as Gerard Manley Hopkins named it, is one way to develop a steadfast heart for the future.

RECEIVE

Be gentle with yourself if you've been repressing angry feelings for many years. Take the time and seek out the experiences you need to grow. "When we don't need to be angry anymore," writes Melody Beattie, "we'll quit feeling angry if we want to."

STEP 5

"SUMMONING" SELF-ACCEPTANCE THROUGH HUMILITY

> While they were talking and discussing together,
> Jesus himself drew near and went with them.
> But their eyes were kept from recognizing him.
> Luke 24:15-16

"SUMMONING" SELF-ACCEPTANCE

ONE OF MY favorite New Testament stories, often referred to as the "Appearance on the Road to Emmaus," demonstrates how steps toward healing and enlightenment cannot be taken when crouched in fear. Two dedicated followers of Christ, fleeing Jerusalem for a nearby town just days after witnessing the Crucifixion, encounter but do not recognize the risen Lord. Perhaps a heightened, emotional state blinded them to the truth of the Resurrection. One of the followers is Cleopas, perhaps Christ's blood uncle. But even he cannot recognize his nephew and is so distressed he lashes out in response to an innocuous question, sharp words most certainly regretted later: "Are you the only visitor to Jerusalem who does not know of the things that have taken place there in these days?" he rebukes Jesus. Not until that evening, when the stranger blesses the evening meal, do the two disciples realize their heart-rending error. At that exact moment, their beloved rabbi disappears from sight.

One of the rewards of Spiritual Reading, especially in the last movements, is discernment—that is, discovering truths revealed in steps called "summoning" and "serving." But even those of us who diligently tread the intentional path of practice struggle to sort through competing messages common during our times of strain.

Under duress, every word can seem a summons, confused thoughts and feelings can be given equal weight with divine promptings or dark calls of deception. Too much analysis can paralyze us. "Never make a decision in desolation" is a well-known maxim in Ignatian spirituality, practiced by members of the Jesuit religious order. Desolation always threatens discernment, just as it did along the Road to Emmaus.

Science explains why this happens. When someone experiences a stressful event, the most primitive parts of the brain, the amygdala and hypothalamus, prompt the urge to fight or to flee. In fact, the emergency wiring of the nervous system is so efficient, the body reacts before the mind can catch up. A cascade of hormones is dispatched to muscles, heart, and other vital organs before the brain's visual centers even have a chance to fully process what is happening. After this initial surge, the emotional center activates a second response system aimed at keeping the body alert—muscles tense up, breathing becomes shallow, the pulse quickens—all anticipating the next threat. Even low levels of stress, when chronic—common if living with an addict—can keep a body on high alert at all times.

"Many of us react as though everything is a crisis because we have lived through so many crises that crisis reaction has become a habit," therapist Melody Beattie observes of those in enmeshed relationships. Often below the level of consciousness, we become so afraid of what has happened, what might happen, and what is happening that even the

"SUMMONING" SELF-ACCEPTANCE

smallest spark can ignite a conflagration and we rush to put out the fire without thinking. "We may stay so busy reacting," Beattie adds, "that we never have the time or energy to identify the real problem, much less figure out how to solve it."

Years of prepping airtight rationales and steeling myself for disagreement over every household decision shared with my children's father, ranging from who would transport them to school to when it was time to purchase a new refrigerator, gave me a kind of battle fatigue, with symptoms common to those of shell-shocked soldiers: disconnection, indecision, and an inability to prioritize.

Years of steeling myself for disagreement gave me a kind of battle fatigue.

In desolation, we cannot spare the brain power necessary for recognizing truth. Good decision-making is further complicated by addicted loved ones who lie and obfuscate as a coping strategy. They become expert at convincing themselves and others of untruths ranging from "I can stop at any time" to "I'm only hurting myself, not you." I first heard a joke at an Al-Anon meeting, more true than it was funny, that went: How can you tell when an addict is lying? Answer: When their lips are moving.

When caught in a web of lies and denials, loved ones have little choice but to become co-conspirators, keeping secrets and denying obvious truths, even those spoken by wise witnesses met along our path. A brother might say, "I wish she'd treat you better." Or a friend, "Your son expects too much of you." Or a child, "Dad doesn't care about us." As youngsters, my daughters sometimes offered clear-eyed observations about their father's self-centered indifference. My immediate response was to deny their concerns lest the wind of truth tumble our house of cards. Rather than legitimizing my girls' instincts with further questions about why they felt something was wrong, I reacted in a way that taught them to minimize their needs and ignore their feelings…as I so often did.

Each of my daughters made such an observation only once, my attempt to excuse their father shutting down indefinitely the possibility of future perceptive intuitions. Years later, when they were adults, I congratulated them for this early insight and wisdom. They insisted I was crazy, assuring me they had *never* felt nor expressed such concerns.

At one point, confusion over what was true about my own identity prompted me to make an Internet search for a personality test called the "Enneagram." A work colleague told me it had origins in several wisdom traditions—Christianity, Judaism, and Islam—and was used both for spiritual and personal counseling as a means of understanding personality, addiction, relationships, and

"SUMMONING" SELF-ACCEPTANCE

vocation. So I typed my credit card number into a website form of the Enneagram Institute, purchasing their "Riso-Hudson Enneagram Type Indicator." The results were immediate if not surprising to someone who proudly called herself "the fixer": I was Type Two, "The Helper," whose basic desire was "to give and receive love."

Sure I had discovered a magic compass to direct all future steps, I skimmed the explanations. The "vice" associated with my personality type—a word I first learned in parochial grade school—was "pride," one of the Seven Deadly Sins. I realized then that it was pride that made me think I could protect my children and myself from abuse. Pride assured me I could help anyone and everyone, whether or not they asked me to, sure I was the most capable person to take responsibility for meeting their needs. Pride told me it was possible to make others love me and need me. Convinced this new self-awareness was a summons to atone to everyone for everything, I planned and piloted an epic apology tour.

Those with loved ones in addiction recovery have likely been a destination on such a circuit, receiving unexpected apologies by phone, text, or in-person visits. In 12-step programs, this is known as "working" Steps 8 and 9 or "making amends." When done sincerely, the object is not only acknowledging the harm or hurt caused by addiction, but also demonstrating sincerity through action and restitution. I've listened patiently to both sincere apologies and faux-pologies that shift blame, as only addicts can, using what therapists sometimes call "pretzel logic." In all cases, I bestowed forgiveness, something I've always found easier to give than to receive.

Admitting failings to another human is difficult for anyone. When the audience for your *mea culpas* is a virtuous man wearing a Roman collar, it is even harder. I made my first sacramental confession in fourth grade, learning that of all the seven sacraments only the Eucharist and reconciliation can be experienced frequently, even daily. Yet most of my adult life, I avoided queueing up to talk to a priest behind a screen, or worse for me, face-to-face. If the guilt of Lent prompted an examination of conscience, I'd hurry through my time using a script memorized at age 10 and rarely deviated from—confessing no more than two sins and one past sin. This childlike approach to the Sacrament of Penance and the grace of divine absolution didn't mature until a colleague who had converted to Catholicism chided me: "I cannot understand why Catholics avoid confession," she said. "To me, it is just a mini-therapy session. And it is free!"

By then, I was no stranger to therapy, so a fresh approach to reconciliation seemed worth a try. Instead of the set script, I poured out my sins ad lib, to more than one priest, in more than one confessional. The only problem was that no absolution, even that provided by Christ in the person of my confessor, assuaged my guilt and self-blaming.

When I finally accepted that my decision to keep a faulty marriage together because it was what I assumed

"SUMMONING" SELF-ACCEPTANCE

was best for my daughters had in fact injured them, I queued up and confessed the sin of pride again and again. I started an electronic document titled "The Co-Dependent Chronicles" where I noted every time I realized, too late, that I was enabling my first husband by taking on most shared responsibilities as my own. I visited upon each of my girls tearful tallies of these trespasses so many times they begged me to stop.

Unfortunately, even formal amends prescribed by kindly confessors, such as do a good deed, say the Our Father, take a walk, or forgive myself, seemed too tepid and insufficient. Neither did any apology of mine yield the "all is forgiven" embrace I craved.

So I returned to the Enneagram website, discovering that in my reactive state I had overlooked explanations that the test and results were "just the first step" in a lifelong journey toward authentic self-knowledge. This insight also explained why I could never achieve anything near to a contemplative state during my Spiritual Reading, because the last movements of Spiritual Reading summon knowledge of self as we were created to be. "We over-identify with our repetitive thoughts and feelings," the website explained. "Contemplative prayer helps us let go of who we think we are and rest in simple awareness of Presence."

I discovered that each vice in the Enneagram system is paired with a virtue, something identified as a "gift." For example, the virtue of Type Twos like me is supposed to be humility, which the website defined as recognizing human limitations and being compassionate in that knowledge. For most of my life, I had defined humility as denial of my own needs in sacrifice for the needs of others. Though I craved the kind of love and attention I lavished on others, expecting anything for myself seemed selfish—the opposite of humility. Pain, I told myself, was a consequence of unrealistic expectations, such as believing my first husband wished to beat his addiction despite all evidence to the contrary.

> *I had defined humility as denial of my own needs in sacrifice for the needs of others.*

Apparently, I had serious gaps in my understanding. So I chose a text for Spiritual Reading considered by many to be the best on the topic of humility, a memoir titled *The Story of a Soul*.

Thérèse of Lisieux, who died at age twenty-four of tuberculosis in her Carmelite convent in Normandy in 1897, became famous for a child-like and humble approach to spiritual life that became known as "The Little Way." Her book is considered such a significant contribution to theology and doctrine that, in addition to the title of saint, she is also considered a "Doctor of the Church."

The first time I attempted to read *The Story of a Soul* years earlier, nothing much had "shimmered" in the experiences of a cloistered nun, far removed from mine as a working mother. Thérèse's scrupulosity, a pathological anxiety about religious morality, seemed pitiful and self-flagellating to me. I could not understand how she *enjoyed* "aspersions" such as dirty water splashed inadvertently on her face by another sister. I wrote off her example as dangerous and anti-feminist, returning the paperback to my library with disgust and disappointment.

Timing is important when reading with intention, as is reckoning with a text repeatedly, willing to see in it nothing much to savor on one day or one week but returning later to find its insights. At first I returned not to Thérèse's book, but to her legacy. Soon after the young nun's death, the faithful began praying to her for help in discerning tough decisions. After nine days of prayer to her intercession—called a novena—supplicants reported receiving a sign: the unlikely appearance of actual or figurative roses. "My mission—to make God loved—will begin after my death," she wrote in her memoir. "I will spend my heaven doing good on earth. I will let fall a shower of roses." For that reason, Thérèse earned the nickname the "Little Flower."

In desolation, the most difficult decision of my life came with great self-doubt. My therapist promised to guide me through the process of my divorce from an addict who had long exploited such insecurities and weaknesses for his own gain. But I figured it wouldn't hurt to request divine confirmation. Moments after uttering the last amen on the ninth day of prayer to the Little Flower, I noticed for the first time along my usual running route a rose bush in full bloom. Certainly, I had also missed something in Therese's memoir. Later that day, I ordered a personal copy of *The Story of a Soul* from Amazon.

While the first two movements of Spiritual Reading require an inner focus, the third—prayer—is an outward expression. When summoned, we are compelled to respond. However, when words of a text reveal uncomfortable truths—in my case, that my disordered definition of humility had allowed me to be manipulated—the reply can stick in our throats. In those cases, "lectio continua," reading the same text and interpretations of it over several weeks, enriches acceptance. Hard realities are more palatable when chewed slowly, easier to swallow and fully digest.

That we are indeed sons and daughters of the light is a belief that must seep slowly into our psyches, memories, and souls. So that autumn, when I simultaneously filed for divorce and began a new semester teaching college students, I also became a student myself, enrolling in Thérèse's school of humility.

My required text for myself over three months was her book. This time I read with openness—my form of humility. Only then did literal interpretation of the nun's experiences fall away to reveal the metaphysical, the universal. When Therese saw a mystical vision of angels gathering the blood of Christ in shells at the base of the cross, she reported feeling a "pang of sorrow," an emotion I well understood. "The cry of Jesus on the Cross sounded continually in my heart," she wrote. "'I thirst!'" When I read those words every day for a week, they resounded with familiarity. I was likewise parched, both figuratively and literally. Friends began to express concern over my dropping weight and drained countenance.

During recovery from both her own alcoholism and co-dependency, writer Heather King spent a year reading *The Story of a Soul*. In King's spiritual memoir, *A Shirt of Flame*, she observed this about Therese: "On the outside, she was nothing—little; but on the inside she was consumed with love...for God, for others."

With the help of King's interpretation of *The Story of a Soul,* I absorbed rather than analyzed the text. I contemplated rather than counter-argued. Over many readings of Therese not complaining about dirty water splashed on her face, I began to understand why she offered no reaction to an unintentional hurt: both the insult and her forbearance were known only to her—and to God. In that way, she offered a more perfect love to those in her life, a love that could never be returned. By performing the smallest acts of kindness with intentionality, she cultivated for herself and her convent family a world of acceptance, a heaven on earth. "To pick up a pin for love can convert a soul," she wrote. I had been blind to the singular purpose of Therese's sacrifices: to soften the heart and to model for others a perfect love.

In his book *Habits of Freedom*, Jesuit priest Christopher Collins suggests actions—small or, as Therese would say, "little"—offer the best path to discernment in times of stress.

"When I am tangled up inside, even if I know in my head I'm being deceived, what to do?" Collins wrote. "If I just try hard to snap out of it, that won't work. If I just think real hard in my own head, trying to figure things out and convince myself of the truth of things, that won't work either. At least not in my experience. I can't think my way out of these times. I have to keep acting. I have to keep living. Keep doing the next thing in front of me."

Therese kept doing what was in front of her, the most mundane tasks of daily life. The Little Way, I discovered, was never manipulative, never motivated by the ulterior motive of soliciting either internal or external reassurance and affirmation. Months of my reading *The Story of a Soul* failed to uncover in that text a single instance of self-pity and not a whiff of egoism masked as altruism.

"SUMMONING" SELF-ACCEPTANCE

Therese demonstrated to me that if we are beloved by God, chosen and innately valued, no earthly confirmation or validation is necessary. Many of us long for such love, King observed, but "we are also afraid that we're not good enough, not clever enough, not deserving enough." That feeling of inadequacy, she wrote, is especially common among those of us raised in families afflicted by addiction, even if troubled souls lived in far-past generations. In 2014, a seminal book by neuroscientist Bessel van der Kolk launched new research and treatment of what has become known as "inherited family trauma." His book, *The Body Keeps the Score,* documents not only that experiences in childhood and adolescence that seem mild to adults—such as being insulted or endangered by a caregiver or simply witnessing verbal or physical abuse—can jeopardize normal development. Such trauma, even if repressed, finds expression in not only adult behaviors such as addiction and dysfunctional relationships, but also in physical well-being, right down to the genetic level. The fact that five out of seven children in my family of origin married active or recovered addicts seems beyond coincidence, especially considering how my parents were their own families of origin's primary "helpers," who managed alcoholic parents and siblings.

Thanks to Therese's example, I recognized my definitions of both pride and humility were disordered. They had not matured beyond what I learned in Catholic grade school, and I failed to question my understanding in adulthood until suffering great pain from misdirected self-sacrifice.

It turns out that pride is not only "showing off," but also false humility, recognized in contemporary times as a "humble-brag." As Fr. Richard Rohr, one of the first authors to publish books in English about the Enneagram, writes, "When TWOs reach the point where they recognize their real motives ('I give so I can get'), they may cry for days. When a TWO can finally cry tears of self-knowledge, [then] redemption (healing) is near."

I wept bitterly when I read this: "TWOs originally know themselves as the beloved of the universe," Rohr writes of the Enneagram type. "When they cannot maintain this truth, they become manipulative and needy of the love of others to 're-convince' themselves of the truth they already deeply know."

Not until becoming convinced of my authentic worth could I love without wanting or expecting love in return, Spiritual Reading of *The Story of a Soul* taught me. On the road to redemption, the words of Therese sparked a yearning for a different kind of love, summoning me to set aside false humility and the self-righteousness that came along with it.

Another text I consulted regularly in my practice, the *Rule of Life* by St. Benedict, taught an additional lesson about humility: Not only was I no *more* deserving of love than others; I was no *less* deserving either. In the longest chapter of his guide for members of his order, observed today both by both lay Benedictines and monks, Benedict describes humility as a 12-step ladder that reaches heaven. We climb toward the goal by *descending* in humility, not ascending. If a moment of ego impedes our progress, "Always we begin again," he wrote.

Following Therese's example, I now seek out one daily sacrifice, known only to me and not benefiting only those I love but strangers, too. Sometimes that means holding my tongue from complaint or criticism, or I might ignore an unintentional hurt or take on an extra task, always unseen and unremarked. If I am ever tempted to congratulate myself for following Therese's "Little Way," to feel superior, or to expect anything but a softened heart in return for sacrifice, I simply try again the next day. The reward of true humility, Benedict writes, is not the love of others but instead the "love of God, which being perfect, casts out fear."

READ

If you've advanced in your practice of Spiritual Reading enough to allow "wrestling" with a text you did not at first accept or understand, return to it for your meditation time over several weeks. Try *lectio continua* with that difficult text or one of the readings mentioned above. Practitioners of Spiritual Reading sometimes read one text over many days, including different language translations that might offer unique connections.

REFLECT

Consider for a moment that the intentional path through life offers more than one good choice at any crossroads. Spiritual maturity requires choosing the best option with acceptance and never regret. Take comfort in the knowledge that one way is never the right way for every traveler.

RESPOND

If you react to stressful situations by adding more to your "to do" list, find instead ways to, like Therese, infuse humility and love into what you are already doing, including simple, everyday actions for which you seek no approval, even from yourself.

RECEIVE

If your reading surfaces a memory of how you once reacted to a stressful situation "out of character" for you, simply rest in this new self-observation. Accept with love your unique way of being in the world.

STEP 6

"SERVING"
LIMITS ARE LOVE

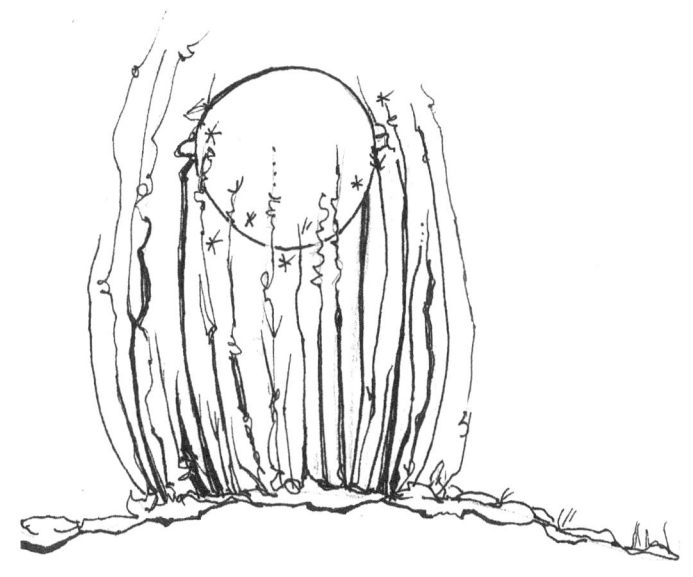

I used to believe that prayer changes things,
but now I know that prayer changes us
and we change things.

Mother Teresa

"SERVING" LIMITS ARE LOVE

HIS VOICE rang out before I saw him, on the second deck of the Staten Island Ferry. "I just visited my aunt, but she wasn't home. I'm homeless. Someone stole all my things. I was stupid. I thought I could handle drugs. I couldn't, but I've been clean six months! I just need seven dollars to shower and get something to eat."

A tall young man with dark hair, half-hidden under a red hoodie, came around the corner, politely repeating his refrain. "Hello, everyone. I am Phillip. Like many 20-year-olds, I had a problem with drugs, but I have been clean six months." He wept, then apologized for his tears as he circled each deck. Most commuters avoided his gaze by looking at their phones or pretending to be engrossed in conversation. I could not turn away from his winsome look and articulate charm, because both reminded me of a beloved nephew who was likewise addicted. My loved one was never reduced to panhandling, always protected by affluence but not by his family's inability to escape the curse of multi-generational addiction and co-dependency. Those associations, and my need to help, made this man's begging impossible for me to resist.

A nearby woman handed Phillip two dollars. I hesitated at first, unsure his story was true. But as he passed, I decided the truth did not matter. I touched him on the shoulder and presented a dollar bill. As his plea echoed from the upper decks, I stared at the Statue of Liberty through a salt-crusted window. I felt like crying: for our country, for all its divided and distracted families, for the addicted and poor, for the forgotten and marginalized. I was in New York City during my spring break to walk in the footsteps of a woman who served them all with a radical love, Dorothy Day.

In the third movement of Spiritual Reading called "Responding," it is possible to receive invitations or opportunities to "serve." As one of my teachers explains, "You may also experience a sense of being pulled or drawn forward into a new way of understanding or into a new action. You may experience God luring you into a recognition of your own deep desires."

Day's voluminous writing—memoirs, newspaper columns, fiction, and biographies—were among the very first texts I explored along my intentional path of Spiritual Reading. Her passion for seeking social change was one I share. For over thirty years, I had worked with homeless causes as a volunteer—in my twenties helping establish in my hometown of Columbus, Ohio, the city's first family shelter. From young ages, my three daughters served alongside me at soup kitchens, food pantries, and shelters.

Like Day, I interpreted the social teachings of our shared Catholic faith as a call to authentic human encounter and service. She was someone who challenged reformers and social activists to maintain their engagement with the Church and the gospel and conservatives to be open and attentive to the radical social dimensions of the gospel. She urged both groups to resolve differences between them with mutual respect and love for "the benefit of the world."

Newly single and my children now grown, I came to New York to discern if and how to reply to what I thought was an invitation to follow in Dorothy Day's footsteps. I hoped to shake off, once and for all, the persistent feeling that I was never serving and helping enough.

Beginning during the Depression, Day established in Manhattan both an alternative newspaper and an intentional community of like-minded souls willing to deny themselves in order to serve the most forgotten. She was both a one-time Communist and a convert to Catholicism who described in her newspaper column the mission of the Catholic Worker organization in these words: "To advocate for those who are huddling in shelters trying to escape the rain, for those who are walking the streets in the all but futile search for work, for those who think that there is no hope for the future, no recognition of their plight." A loose confederation of some 200 communities continues her work today around the world. The local chapter in Columbus had disbanded a few years earlier. During my Spiritual Reading of Day's writing, I felt summoned to help re-establish this community.

So to find out if that was truly my call, I packed a small bag of essentials, booked a flight, found a room in a converted apartment house just a few blocks from the Catholic Workers' main office in New York City inside a women's homeless shelter, Maryhouse. Day had lived there until her death in 1980, just as other "helpers" do today, in solidarity with those they help. The core staff of the two NYC "houses of hospitality" that Day established, including the men's shelter, St. Joseph's House, practiced voluntary poverty. During my short stay working at both, I was both embraced and repulsed, accepted and challenged, and my faith was deepened and shaken.

By the time I disembarked the ferry from Staten Island, where I had visited Dorothy's Day's grave, I was well-versed in the daily routines of serving meals to long lines of men and women, inviting anyone to take as many donated clothes as needed, and otherwise saying "yes" to all requests for help. Day's belief, unique in my experience working in other homeless shelters, was that generosity—rather than rationing of donated resources—would be rewarded with more resources that would be provided with providential timing. So when one man and his young son arrived too late for the afternoon meal, we gave them a full jar of peanut butter and an entire loaf of bread. That week I experienced firsthand what it meant to see in the faces of the poor the face of Christ. After the first four days working in Day's shelters, I was more convinced than ever I would establish a house of hospitality in my hometown.

Departing the ferry from Staten Island on the fifth day, I was swept along in a crush of commuters to a packed, uptown-bound train. When a suited man offered me his seat, I accepted immediately, but then heard a soft voice from the seat next to mine: "I'm sorry, M'am, that I didn't get up right away. I didn't see you." Turning toward the apology, I saw only a red hoodie. "Phillip, from the ferry!" I exclaimed. He smiled, revealing a shocking mix of black, jagged, and missing teeth, a sure-sign of a methamphetamine addict. As the train sped toward the Lower Eastside, we chatted honestly about how addiction touched our lives and the work of St. Joseph's House.

"I love the Catholic Worker," Phillip assured me as the brakes squealed to another stop. "They are like family to me," he added as he grabbed the stanchion and stood. "I can tell you I would not be sober at all were it not for them." Leaning his hooded head close to my head, he asked my name. I replied and promised to remember him to the staff at the men's shelter. Then, as the doors whooshed opened, familiar words crossed my lips, perhaps the first time in my life, at least to me, sounding sincere: "I will pray for you," I said.

"Thank you," he mouthed and exited.

In the Serving step of Spiritual Reading, sometimes our habitual ways of being come into question, forcing us to soften our hearts with new compassion to ourselves, others, and all of creation. For my reading that week, I had chosen a newly published biography of Day authored by her oldest granddaughter, Kate Hennessy. *Dorothy Day: The World Will Be Saved by Beauty* confirmed biographical details I already knew, including those that made the Worker foundress an especially controversial figure among conservative factions of her faith. They point out that before her conversion to Catholicism, Day had an abortion, made two suicide attempts, and mothered one child without ever marrying her daughter's father. Even after her conversion to Catholicism, she remained a radical pacifist (even to World War II) and she was often jailed in service to her principles.

From the intimate perspective of immediate family, Hennessy also offered new insights, ones in conflict with my long-held notions of Christian motherhood. Day's dogged dedication to social change came at a cost. She often deferred responsibility for her only child's upbringing to others. Her rigid adherence to the Church's prohibitions against divorce and contraception meant she expected her daughter, Tamar, to endure personal and economic hardship from her marriage to an alcoholic and raising nine children. Often harsh and unyielding, Day expected her extended family to live as she did—in austere Worker communities. As another granddaughter, Martha, told me during my time at Maryhouse, both her grandmother's love and her faith were fierce. "[That] always sort of scared me," she confessed.

Radical allegiance to high-minded principles isn't for everyone, a lesson I learned at the women's shelter. On Thursday, as the only volunteer near the entrance when a woman knocked and asked for access to a hot shower, I invited her in without question. But I was unsure what to do next. Rummaging through a nearby storage room, I found soap, shampoo, and a change of clothes likely to fit her. Handing them to her, I smiled and said, "Here you go, dear." Both the guest and I were startled as a booming voice resonated from the space behind us. "She has a name, damn it," someone raged. "Don't you *dare* call her 'dear'!" We both turned to see, coming down the hall as fast as her cane would allow, the formidable Jane Sammon, a veteran volunteer and former travel companion of Day's. Inserting her girth between us, she faced me and barked, "She doesn't need your classist condescension." I winced, recalling how often Day characterized her mission as "Comforting the afflicted and afflicting the comfortable." Despite all my attempts to pretend otherwise, I knew I was being counted among the comfortable, a do-gooder volunteering for just one week before returning to a privileged life. Fighting back hot tears of embarrassment, I apologized and asked the woman's name. It was "Kay."

I once heard a long-time Worker characterize himself and others in the community as those who "do nice things, but we are not nice people." I believed it that day.

During the practice of Spiritual Reading, we are often "instructed and corrected," writes spiritual teacher Michael Casey. Especially in the last steps, we must move from the inner world of meditation to an outward focus of action and service, where not all insights are palatable. After all, he adds, the goal of achieving contemplation is not "self-enhancement," but "yielding of our lives into the control of Another."

The next day I was force-fed another slice of humble pie. When sharing with a staffer my meaningful encounter with Phillip, I expected congratulations for my enlightened understanding and demonstration of the Worker-informed principles of mercy and acceptance. Instead, I was eviscerated. "He told you he's been clean six months?" the Worker scoffed. "More likely six hours. He's always scamming…I'll be surprised if he is still alive next week."

I was stunned, ashamed of my obvious gullibility, even more remarkable given years' experience with my own addicted family and friends. My addicted nephew was notorious for sharing well-acted sob-stories to garner sympathy and support of all kinds. Only later, and after much therapy, did I realize why he chose me and a handful of other kin as frequent targets. Those in committed or unresolved relationships with active or recovered addicts are powerless against such emotional manipulation, even if or when they realize the game intellectually. Our lost relative understood not only who was likely to help again and again, but also how easy it was to appeal to a disordered need both to take care of others and congratulate ourselves for doing so.

That nephew once telephoned me from Ireland to report, tearfully, that he had returned to our shared faith during an extended trip. But do not tell anyone, he added. And no, in the land of the pub, he was not drinking. For weeks I listened to and encouraged him, or more accurately enabled him; I was flattered to be taken into the confidence of someone I loved.

If helping anyone and everyone was my primary value, there was no distinction between my needs and those of my beloveds. I had no boundaries. "Caretaking, whether it involves other people taking responsibility for us or us taking responsibility for them, damages boundaries," writes Melody Beattie in *Beyond Codependency*. "It leaves us with an unclear sense of ourselves and others—of who we and others are."

After my two serious scoldings in New York, I likewise doubted my definition of service. As a wife, aunt, mother, co-worker, friend, I gave too much. As a Catholic Worker, I could not give enough. Rather than fly home that Saturday as planned, I sentenced myself to a penance of one more sleepless night in my bedroom where young carousers left nightclubs at all hours just outside my window to a symphony of shouts and breaking beer bottles. I needed more time to understand an emerging truth: that no amount of helping damaged humans would yield the love and respect I craved.

Unmoored for hours that evening, I alternated between reading in my room and wandering the streets of the Bowery, searching for a sense of belonging and a way forward. Late into the night, I finished packing and then opened the Day biography one last time. I propped two stiff pillows against a rickety headboard, took several deep breaths, then skimmed to the end of Chapter 25 in search of words that might shimmer with renewed hope for me. Though Hennessy's portrait of her grandmother was unflinchingly honest, it was loving at the same time. The granddaughter admired her matriarch's strength, love, and authentic humility. "Christ understands us when we fail," one quote from Day declared. "And God understands us when we try to love."

I stopped and re-read that passage, accepting the invitation from my spiritual heroine to sit in tension, to accept without judgment the co-existence of both good and evil in all families and inside each one of us. I considered how Day's definition of love included compassion, not just toward others, but also toward oneself.

When I transitioned that night from meditation to contemplation, I was summoned to consider how helping with few boundaries is not helping at all. As Eugene Peterson wrote in *Eat This Book: A Conversation in the Art of Spiritual Reading*, I moved from "looking at the words of the text to entering the world of the text. As we take this text into ourselves, we find that the text is taking us into itself. For the world of the text is far larger and more real than our minds and experience.... Meditation enters into the large backgrounds that are not immediately visible, that we overlooked the first time around."

In the world of that particular text, I meditated on how my desperate attempts to help my daughters by shielding them from all harm had in fact robbed them of both responsibility and agency. I had cleaned up every mess, both those created by the neglect of their father or by their own. For too long I micro-managed every aspect of their lives and our household. It was no wonder they accused me of abandonment when I eventually moved out and stopped serving them altogether.

In an uncomfortable inn in Manhattan's Lower East Side, a text and the events of the week served me well. What I thought was a call to virtue was, in fact, something darker: a temptation to bury myself in self-righteous service. Even Day had something to say about that. "Dorothy never said everyone should work on the soup line," Hennessy wrote. "[Dorothy said] 'The older I get the more I feel that faithfulness and perseverance are the greatest virtues, accepting the sense of failure we all must have in our work, in the work of others around us, since Christ was the world's greatest failure.'"

As I breathed in those words, I closed my eyes and rested, served by the text. I accepted failure: I was no better than the addicts in my life because helping was *my* drug of choice. I decided it wasn't enough to be more selective about who I helped and how; I needed to stop helping all together. That would become my new boundary, at least for the near future.

"The purpose [of boundaries] is to gain enough security and sense of self to get close to others without the threat of losing ourselves, smothering them, trespassing, or being invaded," Beattie writes. "Boundaries are the key to loving relationships."

After much practice and many failures, I have learned to explain, without emotion, to active users and fellow co-dependents that I cannot—and will not— help them or join in helping toxic people, unwilling to descend into the pit of extreme empathy. Rather than participate in disordered definitions of love, I drop out of toxic text strings, change the subject of conversations that veer sideways, turn down invitations, and otherwise let go of the temptation to feel good about myself by helping as a first instinct. As I protected this perimeter, especially with family, my defenses became impervious to both self-doubt and testing by someone who might say, "Oh, he is not that bad," or "She promises not to get high around you." No longer needy of reassurance and validation, I completely changed how and why I serve.

My boundaries have held fast because their only ambition is to help me, not others. As Lysa TerKeurst writes in *Good Boundaries and Goodbye: Loving Others without*

"SERVING" LIMITS ARE LOVE

Losing the Best of Who You Are, "Setting boundaries from a place of anger and bitterness will only lead to control and manipulation. Setting boundaries as a punishment will only serve to imprison us. But setting boundaries from a place of love provides an opportunity for relationships to grow deeply because of true connection."

After I learned to stop helping, something remarkable happened: emotional manipulators were no longer attracted to me like a magnet. I seemed to repel addicts, and those enmeshed with them, using the force of mutual respect. By asserting the freedom to manage my own relationships, I left them free to do the same. Inside that no-man's-land created by mutual boundaries was my opportunity to focus energy, time, and love differently. I chose instead to offer intercessory prayer on behalf of those I could not help, which is perhaps the most charitable boundary of all.

After I learned to stop helping, something remarkable happened.

After finishing the last step of Spiritual Reading that night in New York, I closed my book, switched off the light, and whispered a prayer asking Dorothy Day to intercede for Phillip's recovery. I prayed, too, for my nephew, that night and every night after, until receiving the tragic news of his overdose death a few years later. In that tortuous time of grief, I recalled wisdom imparted to me through Day's granddaughter, refined into gold in the crucible of family: I had done all I could do. "The wonderful thing is that each one of us...can go only as far as the grace of God leads," [Day once wrote]. "God 'ordereth all things sweetly,' so there is no need to be afraid."

READ

The following scriptural passage, frequently selected for Christian wedding ceremonies, is so familiar it is often interpreted too narrowly. Consider how Paul's love litany outlines what you should expect others to give *you*, not just what you should give *others*. Mutuality is necessary for love to draw us closer to one another...and to God. Love should never tear us apart inside.

> Love is patient;
> love is kind;
> love is not envious or boastful or arrogant or rude.
> It does not insist on its own way;
> it is not irritable or resentful;
> it does not rejoice in wrongdoing,

"SERVING" LIMITS ARE LOVE

> but rejoices in the truth.
> It bears all things,
> believes all things,
> hopes all things,
> endures all things.
> Love never ends.
> 1 Corinthians 13:4-8

REFLECT

If the love you receive is unlike what Paul describes, consider how a new boundary might help. "Anger, rage, complaining, and whining are clues to boundaries we need to set," writes Beattie. "The things we say we can't stand, don't like, feel angry about, and hate may be areas screaming for boundaries." Might you establish one new limitation on what you understand as love? How might setting this boundary through Spiritual Reading guide you in a new direction along the intentional path?

RESPOND

Think of one boundary you have tried to establish and maintain in the past. Reflect on any positive outcomes you experienced. How can your past success (or at least efforts) help you establish clearer boundaries going forward?

RECEIVE

Accept this insight from Christian author Lysa TerKeurst, who made the decision to divorce an addicted spouse. "Please know: It's not unchristian to set these healthy parameters. It's not unchristian to require people to treat you in healthy ways. And for us to do the same for others. It's not unchristian to call wrong things wrong and hurtful things hurtful. We can do it all with honor, kindness, and love, but we have to know how to spot dysfunction, what to do about it, and when to recognize it's no longer reasonable or safe to stay in some relationships.

STEP 7

"SLOWING" ADJUSTING TO NATURE'S PACE

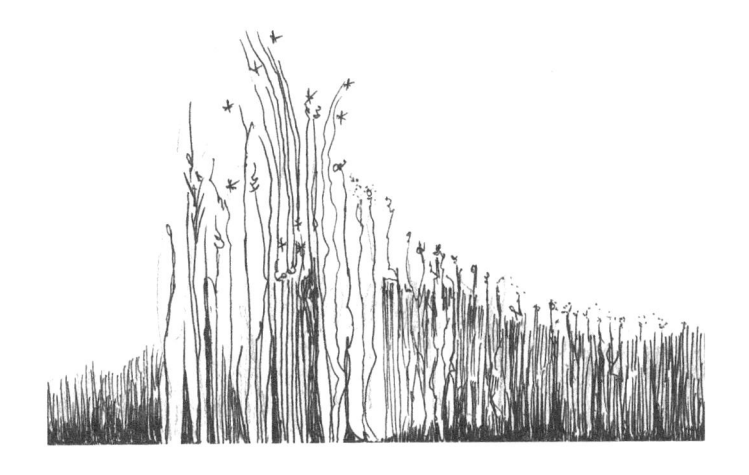

In order to master changes,
we have to recover slowness, reflection, and togetherness.
There we will find real renewal.

Guttorm Fløistad, "Slow Movement" Manifesto

"SLOWING" ADJUSTING TO NATURE'S PACE

WHEN SHE spied one slender stalk topped by a scaly tip, my young daughter squealed and clapped gloved hands. The sprout had emerged just one inch, virtually overnight, stretching above a tangle of dry stalks, melted snow, and dead leaves at the northern edge of our family garden. This arrival had been anticipated for weeks, practically forever on the calendar of a three-year-old.

From the time she could toddle between furrows, my first child and her sisters after her wielded colorful trowels alongside my spade and hoe as we planted and harvested everything from cucumbers to cantaloupe and green beans to grape tomatoes, often plucked, brushed against a shirt, and consumed on the spot.

As fellow nurturers, the girls learned to be alert to even the slightest sprouting. But the vegetable spotted by my oldest that late March was unique among all the leaves, fruits, and roots consumed annually from our backyard garden: the asparagus had been planted before she was born, but could not be harvested until that season.

From as early as I can remember, I hurried—thinking fast, talking fast, walking fast, eating fast. Patience is a virtue, but not mine, until I was required to accept the pace of nature. From the moment I first indulged the human impulse to cultivate — caring for fellow humans or flora and fauna—I signed a contract with an immutable timeline. New life of any kind, growing inside a human body or coaxed from the earth, emerges slowly, according to a cosmic clock and without regard for even the most intense impatience. Anyone who has taught or mentored anyone, whether a child or an employee, knows that attempts to rush maturity imperils the end results: both meaningful growth and the satisfaction of witnessing it firsthand. Nature, both human and environmental, goes slow.

In the practice of Spiritual Reading, transitioning from meditation—summoning and serving, to contemplation—slowing and stilling, cannot be forced nor rushed. We must lose track of time, just as we do whenever we are immersed in an activity we love. When in the garden, I mark minutes only by the position of the sun relative to the scale of my ambition for the day. In that way, I experience a bit of eternity. Timelessness is an enticement to go slow, to surrender my agenda.

After a wedding at what I thought was the wise age of thirty-one and purchase of a home on nine acres, I spent years immersed in planning, plowing, and planting new beds for flowers and vegetables. The yard had once been a soybean field, still weedy and willful, but it had one overriding advantage: full sun. So I studied and strategized, investigated and invested, not only in annuals with short-lived bursts of color and fragrance but also in sturdy shrubs, flowering trees, and plots of perennials whose full beauty blossomed only after successive seasons of care and maintenance. I'd brave the weather of all months to check, coax, and coddle my crops, delighting in even the smallest developments.

"SLOWING" ADJUSTING TO NATURE'S PACE

Convinced my family's roots were also planted permanently on that property, after a few seasons I dedicated a four-foot-square section of the plot near our garage to asparagus. That spring of 1998 was my first as a true Earth Mother, both confident in the ability of my plants to produce in a far-off future and in my body's capacity to knit and bear another human by year's end. Both endowments promised the security I craved and the patience I needed. From slowness came sagacity. From restraint, reward. As the poet Rachel Pritchard wrote while awaiting the birth of her daughter:

> There's no hurry.
> We're just relaxing
> In this golden pregnant time
> This pause... just hers and mine.

I raised my own daughters on oft-repeated tellings of the asparagus origin story, always married with their own. "Once upon a time," I'd begin with each of them, "before you were born, I dug a trench, filled it with compost provided by our horses, and then secreted, deep in the dirt, an octopus-shaped root called a crown. I watered, tended, and abided it for four years, allowing the roots to develop over several winters so stalks would one day grow sturdy and full of possibility. Likewise, I waited nine months for your arrival, as you grew stronger and smarter inside me, unseen but already loved."

To assure perennial plentitude of nutritious harvest for years to come, I left young asparagus plants to flourish until they, willowy cousins of the houseplant known as asparagus fern, feathered. Even after maturity, I refrained from harvesting every spear, leaving the thinnest and thickest behind to recharge rhizomes hiding in the dirt.

"Sometimes we must trust nature's clock over our own," I told my children. The point of the planting parable every time was that "good things come to those who wait." And because they were each a wanted, an awaited, darling daughter of God, they were good indeed.

To this day, nothing centers and slows me faster than feet on earth and skin in sun. Immersion in the natural world, whether a garden or a gorge, has provided spiritual connection for centuries. "Creation is the song of God," wrote medieval abbess Hildegard of Bingen, also an herbalist and healer. She taught that being out of sync with the beauty and fecundity of nature is to deny the force which enlivens body and soul. She called this force *viriditas*, the Latin word for "greenness." We are not above nature, but an intimate part of it. In the wonder and splendor of nature, she saw a divine underpinning that sustained not only the earth but also the cosmos.

Gardening offered all my daughters and me a pace unchanged and eternal, natural and sublime. We went slowly. I resisted culture's push on parents to make children's calendars as cluttered as their own, opting instead for Saturday afternoons fashioning crowns of clover for our hair, walking in the woods behind our home, and swinging on a hammock with barn cats on our laps or a grazing horse alongside.

So often has the pace of modernity taxed the ability of humans to keep up that history is full of "slowdown" reform movements and cultural shifts, both spiritual and secular. Buddhist monastics retreated to the desert to pursue a life of "slow thought"—meditation—over 2500 years ago. In the fourth century, Catholic monasteries made space for prayer, silence, and reflection seven times a day by praying the Divine Office. My back-to-earth, grow-my-own asparagus impulses emerged from the Slow Food Movement of late 1980s, which spawned slow movements in almost every aspect of culture, from cinema to city-life, gaming to gardening, and fashion to faith. It is now sometimes known as "new monasticism."

Carl Honoré, in 2004's *In Praise of Slow,* characterized the movement as a "cultural revolution against the notion that faster is always better. The Slow philosophy is not about doing everything at a snail's pace. It's about seeking to do everything at the *right* speed. Savoring the hours and minutes rather than just counting them. Doing everything as well as possible, instead of as fast as possible. It's about quality over quantity in everything."

One benefit of quality use of time is consideration. For example, first-time visitors to present-day monasteries are sometimes surprised by how slowly monks chant and how often they pause between readings and prayers. The silences are intentional, of course, to allow reflection. Slowness allows "discernment," the ability to think clearly, set goals, and determine the best way forward without rushing. Ignatius of Loyola taught his followers to "never make a decision in desolation," that is, any time when anxiety and pain make objective perspective unlikely. His "Daily Examen" guides self-reflection at midday or evening or both. The steps include first, realizing a holy presence; then, expressing gratitude; next, reviewing the day's events with that presence's help; then finally, admitting shortcomings and asking forgiveness—until looking forward to the next day considering all that was learned. Just as in Spiritual Reading, fruits of this method are achieved not by analysis but by release of expectations. In a place of surrender and acceptance, better decisions to act—or permission to *not* act at all—arise.

Unfortunately for me, before learning the importance of surrender from 12-step recovery, my desolation increased as my daughters grew older. By the time they were middle schoolers, it became impossible to dispatch them to bed before their father's pints, peevishness and passive-aggressive pitch-battles began. I turned to structure and standards to shield them instead. With charts and schedules, I planned all aspects of their lives, from media use to music practice, from schoolwork to barn work, from food to fun. My rearing and our relationship grew as hard-edged and thorny as the honey locust trees growing in our backwoods. Only years later did I understand their anger when I dropped all of that control and moved out, accepting slowly their accusations of abandonment. "Believing lies, lying to ourselves (denial), chaos, stress, low self-esteem, and a stomach full of repressed emotions may cloud our ability to think," writes Melody Beattie about the consequences of living too long with addicted loved ones.

In healthy families, "unparenting" happens organically, timed in accordance with maturation. But in families marred by addiction, divorce, or mental illness, children are often wrested from parental care before either party in the relationship is ready. My leaving my children to grow on their own was a harvest hard to swallow until, through Spiritual Reading, I learned to scale back my need for affection to be returned by them.

My leaving my children to grow on their own was a harvest hard to swallow.

Just as asparagus sprouts must multiply and manifest before any one harvest can make a meal that satisfies, my disordered relationships would need to lie fallow even if my appetite for love remained. The true source of that love, in my belief, was God, not my children. Making room for that love required I end not only my season as a caretaker of an addict, but also my period as an over-nurturing parent. I explained to my daughters that because I loved them unconditionally, forcing us to be a family would choke the growth of any enduring relationships. Although we lived in the same city, three consecutive Mother's Days passed without celebration, and other holidays and birthdays were only acknowledged by mailed greeting cards or text message exchanges. I waited. I slowed, rarely communicating unless and until they initiated a conversation. Before indulging any deep-seated instinct to advise or attend, parent or plan around my progeny, I did nothing instead. As Dennis Wholey writes in his book about alcoholism, *The Courage to Change*, "Waiting is an art…waiting achieves things. Waiting can be very, very powerful. Time is a valuable thing. If you can wait two years, you can sometimes achieve something that you could not achieve today, however hard you worked."

In the meantime, I cultivated goals all my own and the confidence to achieve them without guilt. I learned to think again. Just as I allowed feathery asparagus ferns to take over my garden each June, wither each September, then come back stronger than ever the following March, I trusted that the divine rhythm of rebirth would someday yield a more perfect love, one shared with my daughters and then multiplied a hundredfold.

"SLOWING" ADJUSTING TO NATURE'S PACE

READ

Try walking in nature contemplatively, seeing what shimmers when going slow. Bring full attention and presence to each step, then focus on just one element of your environment, anything from a tiny leaf to a wide-open vista. Even if the minutes seem to drag on, resist the temptation to be satisfied with only momentary gratitude. Lean into slowness until it feels natural.

REFLECT

Next, open your heart to any images, memories, or feelings that stir in you while in nature, welcoming whatever comes. Do not avoid, do not judge.

RESPOND

Consider how the natural world—a garden, a park, a mountain—invites not just appreciation but also a divine response *from* you. Is the way you walk the way you choose, the way you desire? Consider adding slowness to a time of reflection at the end of every day, perhaps following steps of the daily examen.

RECEIVE

When you return from any walk or time in nature, always allow a few moments for stillness. Sit, being present. Take note of how your body feels both after your time of movement and pause, so you are sure to make room for the gifts of slowness in the future.

STEP 8

"STILLING" IN A SPIRITUAL MILIEU

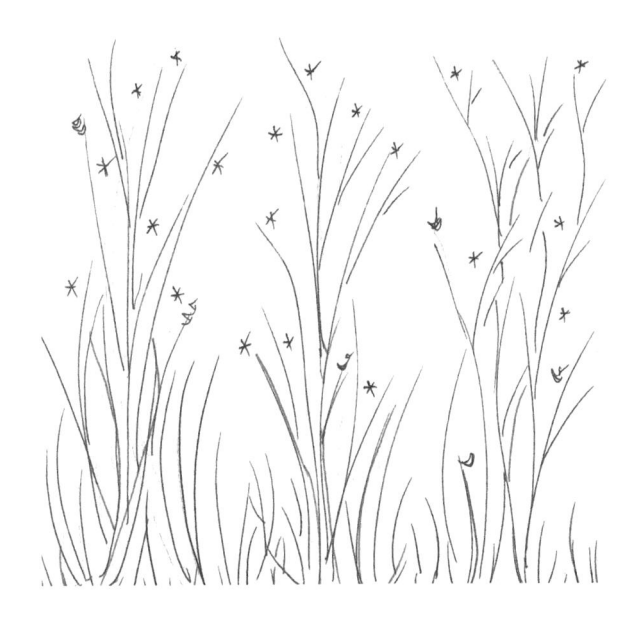

Enter through the narrow gate;
for the gate is wide and the road is easy
that leads to destruction,
and there are many who take it.
For the gate is narrow and the road
is hard that leads to life,
and there are few who find it.

Matthew 7:13-14

"STILLING" IN A SPIRITUAL MILIEU

"RELAX. Waste glorious time with your Friend." "Take naps. Stare out of windows. Allow your mind to slow down. Don't make plans. Don't anticipate the next thing, just be here. Be still. Listen. Let your senses take over and allow God to speak into your heart."

"Whoever reads this, I love you!"

I received seventy messages like these above, tucked inside a red folder and thirty-five more in a white moleskin journal—words of encouragement, advice, insight, and love, hand-printed on postcards, stationery, and random scraps of paper. Some letters were penned in neat, upright cursive, while others were scrawled in messy all-caps. Several included illustrations, quotes, scriptural references, prayers, and one, an original canticle. All were delivered to me across time and the space of intimacy, beginning October 9, 2014, and ending just three weeks before my arrival at the Abbey of Gethsemani the days before Christmas 2022.

Inside a desk drawer in my room, #308, was what one note-writer called a "prayer chain," others "a gift," originating with a humble piece of notebook paper deposited inside the room's Bible by Maria E. of Mentor, Ohio. Or perhaps credit goes to Susan R. of Lexington, Kentucky.

Several correspondents speculated about the identity of the first messengers, but to me, their identity mattered much less than their message: we all deserve and need stillness.

Even years after detaching completely from the toxic relationship with my first husband, I found myself unwillingly enmeshed in other co-dependent relationships, pulled over along the road of healing by anyone inclined to enforce disordered laws of love. Eventually, I came to recognize these entanglements as ditches rather than detours, but serious enough problems to require my attention. So when resources permitted, I'd schedule regular tune-ups, retreating alone in any way possible. My plan for this weekend in the remote Kentucky monastery was to get work done: reading and writing, alone and in silence. I did not expect to be joined by a *community* of solitude, a rest stop shared with fellow travelers, all of whom had moved on.

Before the openness I cultivated through the ancient practice of Spiritual Reading, I may have judged or ignored the advice of these unseen mentors. But trusting the providential alignment of my residence in this special room, I took their direction willingly. I resisted the urge to accomplish tasks my mind had devised, leaving my imagination open to possibility instead. I did nap. I took walks with indeterminate destinations. One ramble led past the grave of Fr. Louis (Thomas Merton), which reminded me how stridently the monk spoke out against the cultural push toward constant productivity.

In Merton's eyes, compulsion toward busyness denied not only individual bodies and spirits rest and renewal but also endangered the body public. When all of us are overwhelmed with daily concerns, he said, we cannot discern solutions to the complex problems of our age. "To allow oneself to be carried away by a multitude of conflicting concerns, to surrender to too many demands, to commit oneself to too many projects, to want to help everyone in everything" he wrote in *Conjectures of a Guilty Bystander*, "is to succumb to violence."

Focusing on who we are rather than what we are to do is the challenge of the eighth and last stage of Spiritual Reading. Compared to the first three movements, which focus on understanding and response, contemplation acts as a counterbalance to action. An openness to mystery allows discernment for both individuals and the collective.

Despite now understanding contemplation intellectually, emotionally, and spiritually, I still struggled to set aside my compulsion to "do," to improve myself by myself. Ready to fuel that impulse were many on-line gurus and social media darlings pushing self-improvement through "mindfulness" apps, all easily accessible through the privacy of my phone and prescribed as the "portals to happiness." A recent Pew Research study noted that Millennial and Gen-Z consumers are fueling a personal-well-being fad. Those two groups are outspending their elders by two times in money (and presumably in time) on life coaching and self-help apps. In other studies, individuals in these groups also report feeling high levels of isolation. Yet these are also the very generations opting out of brick-and-mortar faith communities and the communal spiritual practices they provide, which have traditionally afforded spiritual seekers a means of feeling connected.

Feeling disconnected, even adrift, is often a consequence of enmeshment in disordered relationships. Isolation can be imposed by manipulative loved ones or self-imposed as a way to keep up appearances. A resulting hyper-independence is recognized by therapists as a response to emotional or physical or spiritual trauma.

Seeking self-fulfillment in isolation from others or lacking belief in the Divine reduces the contemplative lifestyle to "a handy little practice for feeling good, but without the ethical and transformational demands," writes contemporary contemplative and author Carl McColman. "Mindfulness is not contemplation," he explains. "What I love about Christian silent prayer — contemplation — is that it .... goes even further, in that it is grounded not just in wellness or in personal enlightenment but in union with God, union with divine Love. That's what keeps me returning to the silence every day."

"STILLING" IN A SPIRITUAL MILIEU

Dutch-born spiritual teacher Henri Nouwen warned that even the most sincere striving toward enlightenment, if undertaken in isolation, will lead to desolation:

> We cannot live a spiritual life alone.
> The life of the Spirit is like a seed that needs
> fertile ground to grow.
> This fertile ground includes not only
> a good inner disposition
> but also a supportive milieu.

The need for a supportive milieu is tangible, finds contemporary scholar and theologian Linda Mercadante. She studies the growing number of American who profess no faith (a/k/a "Nones") or who identify as "spiritual but not religious," finding that those in both groups self-report serious "spiritual struggles." She concludes that those who insist on walking the path toward fulfillment devoid of union—both with the Divine and with others—fail to meet their existential goals. "Struggles with self-hood will likely remain for Nones, since many people find meaning and purpose in an identity held in common with others.... Even if society becomes less religious, Spiritual-But-Not-Religious people may continue to struggle as those around them consign their spiritual quest to simply one lifestyle among many, rather than a moral exemplar."

There is a historical marker in the middle of a downtown Louisville entertainment district, at the corner of Fourth and Walnut, marking the spot of an epiphany of unity with others experienced by Thomas Merton, who at times lived as a hermit. He described the experience as the beauty of belongingness:

> I was suddenly overwhelmed with the realization that I loved all those people, that they were mine and I theirs, that we could not be alien to one another even though we were total strangers. It was like waking from a dream of separateness, of spurious self-isolation in a special world, the world of renunciation and supposed holiness.... This sense of liberation from an illusory difference was such a relief and such a joy to me that I almost laughed out loud.

Setting aside individuality, Merton later wrote, is a necessary condition for successful contemplation, which he defined as "centered entirely on the presence of God."

The solitary pursuit of holiness relies heavily on individual intellect as a guide. But in the fourteenth century, an anonymous author taught it was possible to reach the Divine without using the mind at all. His book, *The Cloud of Unknowing,* introduced *apophatic* prayer, a method that was wordless and free of all content, including symbols, images, and thoughts.

The idea that "vocal prayer" is unnecessary, that we need only surrender to God's will, appears in the Gospels when Christ teaches his disciples: "Your father knows what you need before you ask." Likewise the author, who became known as "The Cloud," told his students to embrace paradox, surrendering their intellect. He called these lessons the "path of unknowing."

"If you were familiar with this work and knew how much it could help you," wrote The Cloud, "you would never quit, not for all the physical joys and rest this world offers."

"Lift up thy love to that cloud," the Cloud instructed. "Let God draw thy love up to that cloud and strive thou through help of His grace to forget all other things."

Along my own path, a different guide gave a similar lesson about surrender, what she called a "blessing of compassion." My spiritual director, a wise and patient Dominican sister in her eighties, always answered my over-wrought attempts at self-improvement with the gentle reminder to stop trying so hard. More than once she replaced my self-negation with self-acceptance and this prayer: "May the God of compassion be with you, embracing you when you are alone or worried or confused; when your heart is besieged with pain…. May the wellspring of compassion flow deep within you until you know the enfolding of God's love."

I would stumble often, Sr. Marguerite taught me, but God's compassion—and my self-love—would help pick me up, dust me off, and send me on my way again. From compassion blossomed community. When I was disbelieved about abuse and judged for detaching my daughters and their father, I sought out a more reliable support network. Well-chosen social groups, recovery meetings, addiction programs, and belief communities are necessary guardrails along the intentional path, especially when old patterns tempt us into the ditch. In other words, our choice of travel companions through life's narrow gate matters. I was alone in Room #308 that one weekend, but an invisible community left behind breadcrumbs to show the way to authentic contemplation. Mysterious guides provided assurance that I will never travel alone.

God's compassion and my self-love would send me on my way again.

After a few days embracing and enjoying the detours encouraged by my room's letter writers, a passage read in the monastery church called out to me as focus in Spiritual Reading. It shimmered: "Do not worry about anything, but in everything by prayer and supplication with thanksgiving let your requests be made known to God."

Consulting the Bible found in my room, I located the scripture's source. The letter to the Philippians (4:6). The apostle Paul wrote the words in farewell to a community of believers in Philippi. Propping myself up on my elbows, stomach on the bed's thin comforter, I progressed through steps of the practice, becoming completely present to myself and to the Divine's nearness. I suspended all striving, all supplication, all worry, and accepted what was surely divine direction. I read further:

> And the peace of God,
> which surpasses all understanding,
> will guard your hearts and your minds
> in Christ Jesus.
> Philippians 4:7

I reflected on how guarding our hearts and minds aligns with therapists' advice for establishing—and keeping—boundaries when managing difficult relationships. In my experience, boundaries provide balance. "We need to balance our emotional needs with our physical, mental, and spiritual needs," writes Melody Beattie in *Codependent No More*. She continues:

> We need to balance giving and receiving; we need to find the dividing line between letting go and doing our part. We need to find a balance between solving problems and learning to live with unsolved problems.... We need to find a balance between letting

go of our expectations and remembering we are important.

Often the most difficult expectations to release are those we demand of ourselves. I'll never forget the first-clutch of anxiety seizing me when, after two years of bi-monthly therapy, my counselor declared me ready to journey onward without her regular roadside assistance. "How will I know the way, what to do and when to do nothing at all," I asked?

Her answer? "You won't. But as a start, accept that your first impulse will always be wrong. Just do something different." While that was hardly a satisfying answer at the time, with practice I learned to hold back or hold off the urge to act, to do, to control, to—well—to help. I had to move from "less helping them" to "more healing me."

Each pause, each redirection made the next one easier. "Not knowing" became less frightening, the possibility of a wrong turn not only likely but also forgivable.

Alone in my retreat house room that day, I savored Paul's next words. They stirred and summoned me at the same time. "Finally, beloved," he wrote "whatever is true, whatever is honorable, whatever is just, whatever is pure, whatever is pleasing, whatever is commendable, if there is any excellence and if there is anything worthy of praise, think about these things." (Philippians 4:8)

Thinking about "things" that were true and pure, pleasing and praiseworthy made detachment from my daughters truly loving. I practiced positivity and modeled

"STILLING" IN A SPIRITUAL MILIEU

self-compassion. Even when my children chose domestic drama with their dad over the peaceful household I offered, I stayed true to Paul's advice: I praised them at every opportunity. If a daughter asked for advice, my usual response was "Only you know what is best for you," and "You are smart enough to figure anything out."

Such are the rewards of a contemplative lifestyle and the practice of Spiritual Reading, which I recently formalized by becoming a lay associate of a Benedictine monastery. After a year of study and formation, I joined oblates from diverse religious denominations in a community that one monk characterized as seekers "whose hearts are already in heaven." Centuries ago, the Cloud wrote that contemplation "begins on earth but continues in eternity." That is because love never ends.

"When your soul is engaged in contemplation,' says the Cloud, "it doesn't worry or feel doubt. It's totally at peace because it knows exactly what it's supposed to do.... You no longer want to wander from the path."

Achieving stillness in Room #308 at Gethsemani, even for that moment, brought me real peace. In a desk drawer, unseen guides stored, just for me, lessons that echoed those of Christ's disciple. I would do the same.

Finding a pen and paper, I offered an epistle of encouragement and compassion, ending with the timeless words of my teacher, Paul: "Keep on doing what you have learned and received and heard and seen in me. And the God of peace will be with you" (Philippians 4:9).

READ

Over the course of his life, priest, professor, and spiritual director Henri Nouwen (1932-1996) wrote thousands of letters to friends, acquaintances, parishioners, students, and readers of his work all around the world. He believed that a thoughtful letter written in love could truly change someone's life. Because he was always honest and open with his correspondents about his personal struggles—including clinical depression—many considered him a long-distance spiritual advisor. Thanks to almost forty published collections of letters, essays, and reflections, Nouwen continues to offer those on the intentional path of spiritual growth practical, poignant, and relatable guidance. Many of his titles, including the essay collection *Here and Now*, are right-sized for Spiritual Reading.

REFLECT

As you finish this book in your hands, ask whether you are living in what Nouwen called a "supportive milieu." Are you surrounded by objects, places, and community that are "honorable, just, pure, lovely, and gracious"?

RESPOND

If you are not in a supportive environment, consider what changes might lead you toward "loveliness" psychologically, socially, and spiritually. As Nouwen writes, "Although we might not be able to create the ideal context for a life in the Spirit, we have many more options than we often claim for ourselves. We can choose friends, books, churches, art, music, places to visit, and people to be with that, taken together, offer a milieu that allows that mustard seed that God has sown in us to grow into a strong tree."

RECEIVE

Accept as enough even the first-flowering of hope. Trust that the intentional path toward the Divine will lead you to a fertile future.

ABOUT THE AUTHOR

AUTHOR, EDUCATOR, and podcast host Jean P. Kelly believes in the power of stories, both hers and those of others, to heal and restore hope.

Over the last thirty years, her essays, cultural commentary, video lectionary reflections, and journalistic stories have been published in local, regional, and national publications and websites, including *U.S. Catholic* and *Sojourners*. Her work explores the intersections of faith, intellect, and writing and reading as forms of prayer.

As host of the award-winning podcast Read. Pray. Write. Searching for Answers: Finding Grace at www.readpraywrite.com, Jean teaches that Spiritual Reading can heal because it creates the time, space, and grace necessary to achieve authentic self-knowledge, self-acceptance, and self-gift, even in times of desperation.

She is an Associate Professor of Journalism at Otterbein University in Central Ohio where she teaches writing, branding, graphic design, and podcast storytelling. Together with her students, Jean puts faith in action both through service-learning projects in urban neighborhoods and student-directed production of her podcast. She teaches community leaders and students alike that amplifying diverse voices through storytelling can change the world for the better.

As a Benedictine Oblate, Jean lives out the spirit of monastic life with support from her community of St. Meinrad Archabbey in Indiana, with loyalty to the practices of contemplative prayer and Spiritual Reading, especially using texts written by female mystics, and by making frequent pilgrimages, often with her husband, Greg, including many unplanned detours to thin places, holy wells, and sacred shrines, both religious and literary.

ACKNOWLEDGMENTS

IT COMES as no surprise to anyone that though books are written by one person, they are the product of many. What you hold in your hands is a work more than six years in development, profiting mightily from both pain and progress, detractors and supporters, dead-ends and one intentional path toward its fruition. I especially am grateful to all those who follow:

Early readers, including my former journalism students, especially Ally Hurd Bozeka and Elizabeth Livingston McQuade. The most supportive and appreciated reader was former editing colleague, Kristine Gross, who though a talented copyeditor looked past such mistakes in early drafts even when it caused the hand holding her red pencil to twitch.

My monastic community of St. Meinrad Archabbey, especially oblate novice director Br. Gregory Morris, OSB. Monks, priests, brothers, staff, and fellow oblates of many denominations have both challenged and supported me intellectually and spiritually, leading to great personal growth now documented here.

My publisher and editor, Gregory Augustine Pierce, for taking a chance both on a novice book author and an unusual concept for a spiritual memoir, for editing my words with respect, and for the opportunity to collaborate on the many decisions required to successfully reach an audience we both hope will be helped by what I share.

My husband, Greg Ramah, saw my authentic self even before I fully recaptured her. I so appreciate that our personal faith journeys are unique but often converge for deep discussion, respectful acceptance, and abiding love. Greg is always an inspiration to me, not only filling my soul, but also my body and imagination with his caring culinary creations after long days of teaching, writing, and editing.

And though last—actually first—I am grateful to my three daughters for the space and grace they've given me over the years to share, unflinchingly, my story...even when it intersects with theirs. I love you, but I hope you will not read this book until you are ready.

APPENDIX 1

FINDING AND CHOOSING TEXTS FOR SPIRITUAL READING

Your journey of Spiritual Reading is uniquely your own. As you choose texts for the practice, keep in mind that a variety of media and experiences can be the starting point for meditative time—books, art, music, nature, even your own life story. The key is to recognize a prompt that has "excess meaning," a selection that has layers that can be responded to in varied ways and ultimately can connect to concrete and unique moments of your life. In addition to resources sourced in previous chapters, see these suggestions for appropriate titles to try.

ABOUT SPIRITUAL READING

Christine Valters Paintner. *Lectio Divina—The Sacred Art: Transforming Words and Images into Heart-Centered Prayer.* Ave Maria Press, 2011. The author provides both excerpts for practice, along with guidance for using other "texts" for meditation and contemplation, such as personal life stories.

ESSAY AND EXCERPT COLLECTIONS

Esther De Waal. *The White Stone: The Art of Letting Go*. Liturgical Press, 2021. An internationally recognized historian and spiritual writer shares short reflections on leaving what is known and loved for new beginnings.

Carl McColman. *An Invitation to Celtic Wisdom: A Little Guide to Mystery, Spirit, and Compassion*. Hampton Roads, 2018. McColman explores how the spiritual traditions found in Celtic myth, folklore, poetry, and lives of Irish and Scottish saints can be applied in the modern world. English translations of prayers, sayings, and stories alongside the original Gaelic and Irish language offer fertile starting places for spiritual reading, showing how contemporary seekers can learn to walk the path of Celtic spirituality.

Thomas Merton, *The Pocket Thomas Merton*. Robert Inchausti, ed. New Seeds, 2005. A palm-size volume of big insights in short passages by one of the world's most recognized spiritual teachers.

CHRISTIAN SCRIPTURAL TEXTS

Eugene Peterson. *The Message: Catholic/Ecumenical Edition*. ACTA Publications, NavPress, 2016. A "reading" Bible translated from original Hebrew and Greek scriptures and approved by biblical scholars, God's words in conversational English. (Note: All readings for Sundays and Holy Days in the liturgical cycle from this Bible, with commentary by Alice Camille, can be found in the three-volume *This Transforming Word: Cycles A, B, C*. ACTA Publications, 2023.)

New American Bible. World Bible Publishing, 1987. The official translation of the United States Conference of Catholic Bishops for use in the lectionary readings at Mass.

New Revised Standard Version Catholic Edition. Division of Christian Education of the National Council of the Churches of Christ in the United States of America 1989, 1993. The official translation of the Canadian Conference of Catholic Bishops for use in the lectionary readings at Mass.

JEWISH SCRIPTURAL TEXTS

Adele Berlin and Marc Zvi Brettler, eds. T*he Jewish Study Bible: Featuring The Jewish Publication Society TANAKH Translation.* Oxford, 2003. The primary translation for all forms of English-speaking Judaism outside of Orthodox Judaism.

DEVOTIONALS

Heather King. *Holy Days and Gospel Reflections*. Ignatius Press, 2013. Thoughts on select Gospel readings, Feast Days, and notable women in the Bible by a frequent *Magnificat* devotional contributor who is a recovering co-dependent.

Jon Sweeney and Mark S. Burrows, eds. *Meister Eckhart's Book of the Heart: Meditations for the Restless Soul.* Hampton Roads, 2017. Short excerpts from the 14th century mystic, Meister Eckhart, who has influenced a wide range of spiritual teachers and mystics both inside and outside the Christian tradition, including Eckhart Tolle, Richard Rohr, and development of 20th century American Buddhism and the Theosophical tradition.

Judith Valente, et. al. *The Art of Pausing: Meditations for the Overworked and Overwhelmed.* ACTA Publications/Saint Mary's Press, 2013.

POETRY

Gerard Manley Hopkins. *The Gospel in Gerard Manley Hopkins: Selections from His Poems, Letters, Journals, and Spiritual Writings.* Margaret R. Ellsberg, ed. Plough House Publishing, 2017.

Mary Karr. *Sinners Welcome: Poems.* Harper, 2009. This collection by recovered addict Karr leverages humor, but also reflects the author's Ignation prayer practice. The book also includes an essay about how poetry, which relieved the author's suffering in a dysfunctional family, eventually became a language of prayer.

John O'Donohue. *Conamara Blues.* Bantam, 2000. The onetime cleric explores his native place in Western Ireland with a feeling of wonder at the mystery of nature and our place in it. The evocative, musical nature of his language and the essential truths of his insights infuse these poems with meaning rich for repeated Spiritual Reading.

APPENDIX 2

RESOURCES FOR HEALING FROM DIFFICULT RELATIONSHIPS

These resources are meant to supplement—not replace—professional therapy and informal support networks:

Al-Anon, S-Anon, Nar-Anon and others are non-profit organizations offering support for families and friends of addicts of all kinds, with meetings, resources, and publications. All use the Twelve Steps of Alcoholics Anonymous as a structure for understanding and recovering from addiction.

Catholics in Recovery and **Celebrate Recovery** are Christian faith-based groups for the addicted, meant to supplement the fellowship of 12-step groups. They also provide resources, publications, meetings and other support for families and friends of those with addiction.

Co-DA offers not only a variety of fellowship meetings in all parts of the country and internationally, but also resources for learning more about enmeshed relationships.

One Day at a Time, by Alcoholics Anonymous, is a book of daily reflections right-sized for Spiritual Reading practice and helpful for recovery from both addiction and co-dependency.

TEN RECENT BOOKS FOR SPIRITUAL READING

Arias of the Human Spirit
by David Rinaldi

Engaging the Gifts of Growing Older
by Frank Cunningham

The Ever Expansive Spirit of God
by Peggy Johnson

How We Can Suffer Our Sorrow
by Pam Smith

Jumpstarting Your Own Legacy
by Paul Mast

The Merton Prayer
by Steven A. Denny

Seeing Haloes
by John Shea

Such Dizzy Natural Happiness
by Patrick Hannon

Tranquility/Transformation/Transcendence
by Mark K. Doyle

Where God Is at Home
by Irene Zimmerman

**Available from ACTA Publications
www.actapublications.com 800-397-2282
and booksellers everywhere**

ADVANCE PRAISE FOR
*LESS HELPING THEM /
MORE HEALING YOU*

An accessible and necessary spiritual guide for those of us recovering from co-dependency and proximity to addiction. The truth is, even after we've joined Al Anon and read Melody Beattie, we often find ourselves still tempted to do too much. In this book we'll find not only solidarity—Jean Kelly's story was instantly recognizable to me—but an invitation to a simple spiritual practice that helps us be still and open to receiving rather than striving. —Jessica Mesman, associate editor, *The Christian Century*

This memoir may be one of a kind in showing how *lectio divina*, the ancient practice of centered spiritual reading, is a contemporary resource for healing. Each well-explained step invites and inspires you to move forward in practicing for yourself what the author is practicing for herself. —Timothy Coldwell, editor, *Meditations for the Time of Retreat: A Lasallian Home Retreat*

ADVANCE PRAISE FOR
LESS HELPING THEM / MORE HEALING YOU

I thought my extreme desire to please my daughter, who is now in recovery, and to make any sacrifices needed to meet her perceived needs is what love looks like. In fact, I did not know where she ended and I began. Reading *Less Helping Them/More Healing You* took me on a journey of spiritual awakening and healing that I have longed for. Jean Kelly is incredibly relatable, refreshingly humble, and raw with deep emotion in sharing her invaluable insights and strategies for healing ourselves. With a perfect blend of relatable personal stories, expert research, and a true understanding of how debilitating codependency is, this book will resonate with anyone who has experienced its suffocating effects. I especially embraced the opportunity to pause throughout the book for self-reflection and empowerment. The permission and encouragement for readers to embrace *lectio divina* is a game changer. I am eternally grateful to Jean for opening my heart to my own healing. — Tammy Adler Foeller, founder, OpenDoor Women's Recovery Alliance, Columbus, Ohio